LIVING WITH TENANTS

Also by Doreen Bierbrier

MANAGING YOUR RENTAL HOUSE FOR INCREASED INCOME

DOREEN BIERBRIER

LIVING WITH TENANTS

How to Happily Share Your House with Renters for Profit and Security

McGraw-Hill Book Company

New York   St. Louis   San Francisco
Toronto   Hamburg   Mexico

To all of my readers

1 2 3 4 5 6 7 8 9 DOC DOC 8 7 6

ISBN 0-07-005233-6

LIBRARY OF CONGRESS CATALOGING-IN-PUBLICATION DATA

Bierbrier, Doreen.
  Living with tenants.
  1. Rental housing—Management.   2. Landlord and
  tenant.   I. Title.
HD1394.B433   1986   647'.92   86-2784
ISBN 0-07-005233-6

BOOK DESIGN BY PATRICE FODERO

ACKNOWLEDGMENTS

The first edition of *Living with Tenants: How to Happily Share Your House with Renters for Profit and Security* came out in February 1983 published by The Housing Connection—which was me headquartered in my basement.

A lot of very kind people were willing to review the work of an unknown self-published writer and give *Living with Tenants* some much needed publicity. I would particularly like to thank syndicated columnist Jane Bryant Quinn, and

Mort Poulson of *Changing Times*
Carol MacGuiness of *The Washington Post*
Tom Petruno of *USA Today*
Steven Morris of *The Chicago Tribune*
Patrice Johnson of *Black Enterprise*
Donna Larcen of *The Hartford Courant*
UPI's Fred Ferguson
American Library Association's "Booklist"
American Association of Retired Persons
Gray Panthers
National Council on the Aging
U.S. Department of Health and Human Services

The thank-you list in the first edition of *Living with Tenants* included the following people:

Nina Barrett	Evelyn Glatt	Tony Provine
Elaine Bronez	Rick Halberstein	Duane Ragan
Verando Caffo	Ken Harney	Kay Schlueter
Jeffrey Ford	Nancy Johnson	Linda Schwartzstein
Sheryl Furman	Carl Jonson	Resi Strickler
Richard Frank	Benny Kass	Ralph Swope
Perry Gawen, Jr.	Al Lefcowitz	Candace Tapscott
Tom Gentile	Edith Netter	

I'd like to add the names of Zane J. Semander, Dirk Partridge, and Glenn Davis who exchanged "war stories" with me on their experiences with the IRS related to shared housing.

Most of all, though, I want to thank the thousands of people who bought the self-published edition of my first book, sight unseen, through mail order. It was an act of faith in some ways. I am in your debt.

This second edition is being published by McGraw-Hill. (Whew! No more stuffing books into envelopes.) It has been revised and expanded to include updated and more detailed information, particularly regarding the tax implications of sharing your house with tenants and an analysis of state fair housing laws.

And now, on with the book!

CONTENTS

CONTENTS

Contents

INTRODUCTION

So you have given up trying to buy a house because you think you can't afford the monthly payments. Or you have a house but are presently separated, divorced, widowed, or retired, and you find you have "too much house" and not enough income left over after having paid the mortgage, taxes, utilities, and repair bills.

During the past few years, home buyers have been confronted by high mortgage rates, renters have been faced with rapidly escalating rents coupled with a shrinking supply of available rental units, and homeowners have had to dig deeper into their pockets to keep up with the costs of maintaining their homes.

For all these reasons, increasing numbers of unrelated people are doubling and tripling up to rent, buy, or maintain a house. In fact, nonfamily households consisting of more than one person grew a phenomenal 140.4 percent between 1970 and 1979. By comparison, family households increased by only 11.7 percent during the same time span. Some experts predict that the growth of nonfamily households, reported at 3.5 million in 1980, will accelerate during the eighties.

And Census Bureau statistics only capture the number of nonfamily households at one given time—sort of like a snapshot. If the Census Bureau could measure how many people *ever* shared their house with a nonrelated person, the numbers would be far greater than current surveys suggest because people will consider sharing their homes at different times during their lives.

The Advantages and Disadvantages of Housesharing

If you ask anyone who has ever lived with tenants about the experience, you may find that it was unforgettable—either very positive or very negative. Before you decide you want to share a house with others, it is important to understand the advantages and disadvantages, so you can maximize the former and minimize the latter.

Money, of course, is one of the main advantages to having housemates. You will be able to make money in three ways. You will collect a monthly rent; you may require tenants to pay a share of the utility bills; and if you own the house you are sharing, the Internal Revenue Service may allow you to take deductions which could give you a tax break, or at least allow you to offset the rent you collect as income with your rental expenses.

Sharing your house with others, however, has other advantages as well. Tenants can help you with the household chores; they can provide a measure of security if you would otherwise live alone; and they may take in the mail and feed the cat when you are on vacation. Tenants can also play Monopoly with you on bleak Saturday nights and listen to you tell stories about the rotten day you had at work.

The chief disadvantage to living with others is a lack of total privacy. People also tell horror stories about tenants who didn't pay the rent, didn't wash their dishes, didn't pay for their long-distance phone calls made to their boyfriends in Australia, and tenants who had a succession of boyfriends or girlfriends who used the bathroom at three in the morning. There are also tenants who insist on telling *you* in great detail about the rotten day *they* had at work when all you want to do is watch television by yourself.

For me the advantages of sharing my house with tenants have overwhelmingly outweighed the disadvantages. Having housemates made it possible for me to buy and maintain a house at a time when most people told me that my salary was too low to consider buying a home. In addition, tenants have provided countless hours of companionship, clogged plumbing, laughter, and insights into areas—from

Republican fund-raising to Vietnamese cuisine—which I never would have discovered if I had lived alone.

What This Book Is About

In the ten years of sharing my house with renters, I have learned ways to maximize the advantages and minimize the disadvantages of sharing a house.

This book has been written as a step-by-step practical guide to explain how to:

- Select a house to bring maximum rent as well as maximum privacy
- Find and keep responsible tenants
- Establish a fair rent
- Draft a useful rental agreement
- Comply with local zoning ordinances and state and federal laws
- Maintain records for tax purposes
- Devise a tax strategy

This book is divided into four major sections:

1. The House: Selecting a Suitable Residence
2. The Tenants: Choosing Your Tenants with Both Eyes Wide Open
3. The Management: Managing Your Household with One Eye Half Shut
4. The Tax Strategy: Setting Up Your Record-Keeping System

My father told me that there are times in life when you have to pay a "tuition" in order to learn something. He wasn't referring to college. I hope that this guide will help reduce your tuition costs as you learn how to share your house with tenants; and I hope you enjoy the experience as much as I have.

1

THE HOUSE

The Rules of the Game

The first step to sharing your house with renters is to understand the legal rules of the game.

Many people mistakenly believe that it is illegal to rent part of their residence. Actually, in most jurisdictions it is perfectly legal to share your house with a limited number of unrelated people who pay you rent. Your local zoning office can tell you how many renters may legally share a house in your locality.

What is more commonly prohibited by local ordinance is a rental arrangement in which one or more completely separate rental units have been carved out of a single-family house. These separate units are often called "basement apartments," "mother-in-law suites," or, to use the generic term, "accessory dwelling units."

Accessory Dwelling Units

An accessory dwelling unit (ADU) is an independent living area complete with its own separate cooking facilities and bathroom which is subsidiary to a primary single-family residence. An ADU may also have the following characteristics:

1

- Outside entrance for the sole use of a tenant
- Separately metered heating/cooling unit for the sole use of the tenant
- Restriction of the tenant from the use of common areas of the entire dwelling

Each local jurisdiction has zoning ordinances which are different from the ordinances of other jurisdictions, so you'll have to check in your own locality to see if the area you want to rent is defined as an ADU and if it is permitted or not.

Even if an ADU is permitted, local housing codes may have other structural requirements. For example, some codes state:

- If it is a basement unit, the apartment must be at least 50 percent above the ground.
- There must be additional off-street parking for the tenant.
- Ceilings must allow for at least 7½ feet of headroom.
- Windows must be no higher than 44 inches from the floor in the unit.
- There must be a minimum (e.g., 500 square feet) and/or a maximum number of square feet in the unit.

You can find out what your local ordinances say by calling your community's zoning or housing office. You may also want to check on the penalties for violations and assess what's the worst that can happen if an illegal apartment is discovered. In many cases you would simply be asked to stop renting out your apartment.

To be honest with you, despite restrictive zoning ordinances, an estimated 2.5 million (largely illegal) ADUs may have been created within single-family dwellings in the last decade. One expert estimates that some 300,000 such units are being built yearly.

Some jurisdictions are starting to change their ordinances to permit ADUs, particularly in owner-occupied houses, and it is likely that many more localities will change their ordinances to permit ADUs in the next few years.

Such major national organizations as the American Planning Association, the National Council on Aging, and the American Association of Retired Persons support the legalization of ADUs.

Even now, though, many local jurisdictions which technically do not allow ADUs won't enforce their ordinances unless a citizen brings the matter to their attention.

The most likely source of complaints are disgruntled tenants or unhappy neighbors. Tenants may complain if they feel they have been treated unfairly by the owner. Why do neighbors complain? A neighbor may report you for one of the following reasons:

- You have made an outside structural change to accommodate the ADU, and your neighbor finds the addition distasteful.
- Your tenant's car is taking the space where your neighbor usually parks.
- You or your tenant are having noisy parties or are playing loud music which disrupts the neighborhood.
- The yard and street area around the house are unsightly because of litter or because your tenant has dismantled an engine in the driveway.

If you decide to rent out an ADU in your house, make sure you know the law, and do take special care that neither you nor your tenant offends your neighbors.

Other Restrictions

Zoning ordinances are not the only restrictions which may limit your right to rent part of your house. There are also covenants, bylaws, or lease clauses which may contain rules that govern rentals.

Covenants are agreements made by the developer or original owner of an area. You may want to review the covenants of your neighborhood to find out about any restrictions associated with the use of property located in your subdivision. Covenants, like zoning codes, can be obtained at your local government office.

Since condominiums form their own small neighborhoods, condominium associations have a list of regulations known as covenants, conditions, and restrictions (CC and Rs), and some may prohibit rentals. The CC and Rs of condominium associations were probably given to you at the time of purchase. You may want to reread them before you decide to rent out part of your condominium.

If you are currently a tenant yourself and decide you would like to have housemates, look at your lease or rental agreement. Even if the agreement prohibits additional people in the household, you may be able to convince the owner to let you share your residence with others in consideration for a slightly higher rent.

Examining the Rental Potential of Your House

There are three major factors in determining the rentability of your house: *location, floor plan,* and *attractiveness.*

Tenants will find the location of your house to be desirable for many of the same reasons that you do. They, like you, may ask the following questions:

1. Is the neighborhood safe?
2. Is the house easily accessible to workplaces, shopping, and transportation?
3. Is the house near public transportation?

Next, examine the floor plan of your house. The more privacy and amenities you can offer a tenant, the higher the rent you can get. Further, the more privacy your tenant has, the more privacy you will have.

Bedrooms and bathrooms are critical in maintaining privacy. A bedroom may be the one place an individual has total privacy in a house shared with others. If possible, you and your tenant should have separate bathrooms as well. Nobody likes to clean up after someone else in the bathroom.

You can still share your house with a renter even if your house has bedrooms close together and there is only one bathroom. Many houses, including single-story ramblers, ranch houses and colonial-style houses, have three bedrooms clustered around one bathroom. It's still possible to have a renter in these houses, but there will be less privacy for both owners and tenants, and owners should be prepared to charge somewhat less rent.

Ideally, your house will have a bedroom and another bathroom for your renter in an area removed from your own bedroom and bathroom. Two-story cape cod houses and ramblers or ranch houses

4

with finished basements often have bedrooms and bathrooms on two floors, and are therefore well-suited for renters. Houses with split-foyer entrances have marvelous rental potential. When you enter a house with a split-foyer, you can immediately go either up a short flight of stairs to the main part of the house or down a short flight of stairs to a finished lower level which is about the same size as the upstairs.

The upstairs area of a cape cod or the downstairs space of a rambler or a split-foyer may contain a bedroom, bathroom, and sitting room, thereby affording a tenant almost as much privacy as a separate dwelling unit. In many jurisdictions it is legal to rent these "almost separate units" as long as they don't have a separate kitchen in them. (Many jurisdictions do permit extra refrigerators.) Rents for such units, though, may be set almost as high as for a separate one-bedroom apartment.

Attractiveness of the rental area and of the house itself is the third factor to be taken into account when setting rents. Obviously you can charge more rent for a light-filled room which has wall-to-wall carpeting than for a room without these features. You can get more rent for a room in a spacious and elegant house than for the same-sized room in an average-looking house.

Structural Changes

Some owners hope to maximize rent by putting additional walls, toilets, or kitchens into their homes. An addition which is practical and well-placed may indeed increase your rental income, give you a possible tax write-off, and add to the value of your house. For example, you may want to put a shower in the bathroom you have in your recreation room, so you can rent out your recreation room with complete bathroom facilities.

My strong advice to you, however, is *not* to make any structural changes which would make your house look odd. It's not worth it.

I have seen houses with upstairs bedrooms which have been converted into jerry-built kitchens, dining areas made into bedrooms, and toilets placed inappropriately in the middle of kitchens.

I've always wondered what kind of tenant would be willing to live in such a place. Even if tenants could be found, though, I guarantee

5

you that the owners will have a difficult time selling their houses with jerry-built "improvements" unless the price is well below market value.

Beware, also, of spending too much money on renovations. If you will receive, for example, $300 a month in rent for an accessory dwelling unit you plan to have in your basement area and a contractor says it will cost $12,000 to make the conversion, it would take more than 3 years to earn enough rent just to cover the cost of the renovations.

Furnished or Unfurnished?

After you have selected the room or rooms to be rented, decide whether you want to furnish the tenant's living area. My advice is *not* to provide furniture unless you plan to rent to short-term boarders or you have extra furniture you don't know what to do with.

Some owners believe they can get higher rent if they furnish a tenant's room. On the other hand, most tenants already have their own bedroom furniture, and your furniture may just get in the way.

Further, tenants will be less likely to move if they have to make arrangements to haul beds, mattresses, bureaus, chairs, and desks to a new residence.

How to Set Rents

There is no magic formula for setting rents. The geographic location of your residence and the floor plan, spaciousness, privacy, and condition of the rooms you have to offer will determine the amount of rent you can ask.

One way *not* to set rents is by taking your monthly mortgage payment and dividing it among you and the people with whom you plan to share your house. If you have just bought the house and it has high mortgage payments, rent calculated this way will be unrealistically high. On the other hand, if you have owned your house awhile and your mortgage payment is low, you may set the rent too low.

The only way to set a fair rent is to do some homework and find out the going rate for rentals in your area. Look in the Sunday classified section of your largest local newspaper if that is the publication which carries the most ads for rentals in your area. First see how much one-bedroom apartments and efficiencies are renting for in the same geographical location as your residence. The rents you see will generally reflect the highest range of rent you could charge. After all, why would people pay more to share a house if they could get a nice one-bedroom apartment for a lower rent?

Then look in the classified section under "Roommates" or "Houses, Apartments to Share" or "Rooms for Rent" or whatever other category your newspaper uses for people who want to share their homes with others. Then compare the features of the rental in the advertisement to your rental, and find out how much rent is being asked.

Talk with neighbors and friends. Find out what they are paying for rent or what they may be charging renters. Later you may even ask potential tenants who look at your house how your rent compares with other places they have seen.

You should evaluate what you read or hear. Remember that the neighbor who brags that he has a tenant who pays $75 per month more than you intend to charge may have had his place vacant for several months (and lost the rent for all those months) before finding someone naive enough to pay an inflated price.

Usually I suggest that you set your rent slightly below the market rate rather than above it. Although you will eventually find someone willing to pay a higher rent, you may have a vacancy for a while, and the higher rent will not compensate for the missed rent of a 1- or 2-month period.

On the other hand, you may have difficulty finding a suitable tenant if your rent is way below the market rate. Many people looking for a place to rent have a range of rents in mind that they would be willing to pay. If the rent being asked is below that range, they will assume that there is something wrong—that the location is dangerous or that the house is dilapidated. Many prospective tenants won't even bother to check out a place if the rent is unusually low.

How to Prepare a House Information Sheet

You are almost ready to begin looking for tenants. Before you do, though, you may want to prepare a House Information Sheet which contains answers to questions a prospective tenant is likely to ask.

Common questions are:

- What is the average cost of the utilities per month?
- How large is the bedroom? the living room?
- How close is the house to public transportation? to groceries? to shopping?
- What are the bus and/or subway routes, and how often do they run?
- How long does it take to get downtown?

A completed House Information Sheet might look like the one below.

HOUSE INFORMATION SHEET

ROOM	DIMENSIONS
Living Room	15' × 20'
Dining Room	12' × 10'
Kitchen	8' × 10'
Bedroom (Rental)	12' × 11'
Recreation Room	15' × 20'

Average Utility Bills per Month
Gas	$53.16
Electric	28.91
Water & Sewage	11.52
TOTAL	$93.59

Tenant's share at 50% = $46.80

Distance to Public Transportation?	Bus (D3)—2 blocks
	Subway (Red Line)—6 blocks
to Shopping?	1.5 miles
to Groceries?	1 mile
Distance to Downtown?	6 miles or 25 min on D3 bus
	10 min on Red Line subway
Frequency of Bus/Subway Service?	D3—Rush hour, every 10 min
	otherwise, every ½ hour
	Red Line—every 10 min

In order to fill in the House Information Sheet, you'll need to get some information.

To determine the average cost of your utilities, look at your bills for the past year, record the amounts, and divide by 12 months. Then multiply that figure by the percentage you expect your tenant to pay to calculate what the tenant's share of the estimated utility payment will be. If you haven't previously shared your house with a tenant, you'll have to let potential tenants know that utility bills just reflect your own consumption and that the bills undoubtedly will be greater with an extra person in the house.

If you haven't kept receipts, your local gas and electric companies and your county or city office which handles water-sewage billing will often be able to tell you what the charges were per month for the previous year.

You can find out bus and/or subway schedules and routes by phoning your telephone operator and asking for the telephone number of the information office for your public transportation services.

A Special Tip for Home Buyers

I have a special tip for some of you who plan to buy a house and rent part of it out immediately. Advertise and show the house to potential renters even before closing or settlement. If you wait until the day of settlement to begin looking for renters, you might lose 1 or 2 months of rent while you advertise and screen tenants.

To ensure access to the house before you actually own it, insert a clause similar to the following one in the offer you make to buy the house:

Seller shall permit buyer to enter and show the house to potential renters at any time prior to the day of closing (settlement) with reasonable notice to the seller.

If you find a renter before you officially own the house, make sure you add this additional clause to your rental agreement:

This agreement is immediately null and void should closing (settlement) not occur on _____ between
                                   (Date)

_____ and _____.
  (Seller's Name)   (Your Name)

Final Preparations before Looking for Your Tenant

Before looking for tenants, take one last look at the rooms you plan to rent out. Make sure that the house, in general, and the tenant's bedroom and bathroom, in particular, are clean and presentable. Now is the time to paint the rental bedroom if it needs it, put up cheerful curtains, and regrout the tiles in the bathroom.

Then ask yourself, "If I were a prospective tenant, would I want to live here?" When the answer is "yes," you'll know that it's time to start looking for your tenant.

Points to Remember

1. Check zoning ordinances, covenants, bylaws, and/or leases to see if there are any restrictions on renting out part of your residence.

2. Select a house with bedrooms and bathrooms which afford maximum privacy to you and your tenants.

3. Make additions to your house only if they will improve the value of your house, and not just to increase the rent.

4. Set fair market rents based on the going market rate. When in doubt, set the rent slightly lower than the going rate.

5. Prepare a House Information Sheet with pertinent facts about the house.

6. If you are buying a house, try to find a renter before settlement (closing).

7. Make sure that the house, in general, and the tenant's bedroom and bathroom, in particular, are clean and presentable before you look for a renter.

2

THE TENANT

Deciding What Type of Tenant You Want

The first question about tenant selection many homeowners fearfully ask is, "Will I have to take anyone who can pay the rent?" Then they imagine being forced to take in an 18-year-old fellow who wears gold earrings to match his gold shimmy shimmy pants, deals dope, practices on his drums for a job with a rock band, and has a 20-foot pet boa constrictor.

Relax. You can pretty much choose any tenant you want on whatever basis whatsoever if that person is sharing a house with you. The ability of potential tenants to pay the rent is only one of several screening criteria you ought to establish before selecting a tenant.

What criteria should you set? Well, the first step is to decide what category of tenant you want.

There are three broad categories of tenants: (1) The housemate-tenant, (2) the boarder-tenant, and (3) the tenant-tenant.

The Housemate-Tenant

The housemate-tenant shares the whole house with you. Both of you have equal access to the living room, dining room, kitchen, and all other common living areas in the house. Usually housework and gardening are shared. In addition, there is usually a fair amount of social interaction, conversation, and companionship in this arrangement. The major drawback, of course, is that neither of you has maximum privacy.

The Boarder-Tenant

The boarder-tenant, also known as a "lodger," is a paying guest in your house. The boarder has his or her own bedroom, possibly a private bathroom, and may or may not have "kitchen privileges." Boarders in single-family homes often do not have access to the whole house, and are usually only responsible for maintaining their own bedroom and bathroom. Sometimes meals, fresh linens, and house-keeping services are included by the owner in this rental arrangement. There is often only minimal social interaction between a boarder and the owner and, as a result, more personal privacy for each.

The Tenant-Tenant

The tenant-tenant is someone who lives in your house in a separate unit such as a basement apartment. This tenant has his or her own kitchen, bathroom, and living area and often has a private outside entrance. You may not even see your tenant except when it's time to collect the rent.

The floor plan of your house will, to some degree, determine the type of tenant you will have. Houses with a finished lower level are often ideally suited to tenant-tenants. If all your bedrooms are on one floor and there is only one bathroom in the house, you may decide to have a housemate for a tenant.

Before you begin to advertise, then, decide what type of tenant would be most suitable given the floor plan of your house and your own personal preferences and lifestyle.

How to Ensure Tenant Compatibility

The next step is to decide what personal traits you will look for in a tenant. If you are going to be sharing the same house with someone, you must find a person who is compatible with your lifestyle and sense of values—or at least not incompatible with you. Analyze your own attitudes and determine what characteristics you would prefer in a tenant. Be honest. Do not assume that you can get along with anyone.

Many people prefer to share a house with someone of the same sex. I know that I do. All my housemates have been women. Although if my house had a separate apartment, I might want to rent it out to a fellow.

Age, too, is often an important criterion in tenant selection. A senior citizen may not want to have an 18-year-old housemate, and vice versa. On the other hand, there have been successful shared housing arrangements between people of different generations. Sometimes a younger person may take on the household chores for an elderly homeowner in return for a reduced rent.

Beyond sex and age preferences, decide how important it is for you if a tenant smokes, owns a pet, or would stay home during the day. In addition, you may have definite opinions regarding the use of alcohol or drugs, boyfriends or girlfriends staying overnight, the use of waterbeds, and what constitutes an equitable distribution of household responsibilities.

Although you can screen for some characteristics in your advertising and over the phone, you may want to wait until you are seriously considering someone as a tenant before asking about more intimate personal habits—for example, if someone plans to have boyfriends or girlfriends sleep overnight. You may also want to be pickier if you plan to share your home with a housemate than if you will rent an accessory dwelling unit to a tenant.

It is essential to set some selection criteria, but remember that you may have a difficult time finding someone if you require potential tenants to meet too many rigid specifications.

The Fair Housing Law of 1968 and Tenant Selection

The main piece of federal legislation which prohibits discrimination in housing is the Fair Housing Law of 1968 which bars discrimination based on race, color, religion, sex, or national origin in connection with the sale or rental of most housing.

The 1968 law, however, does not apply to

rooms or units in dwellings containing living quarters occupied or intended to be occupied by no more than four families living independently of each other, if the owner actually maintains and occupies one of such living quarters as his residence.

Many people don't realize that owners are allowed to screen on any basis not prohibited by law. In other words, an owner might seek a tenant who is a vegetarian, discriminate against smokers, reject someone who works a night shift, and require that a person has lived at least 1 year in a previous residence and has good references from previous landlords.

To give you an example, there was a case in New York in which an owner refused to rent an apartment to a black, single, female attorney on the grounds that he was afraid she would litigate on behalf of tenant rights should she move in. She sued the owner and lost, because she was unable to prove that she was being discriminated against on grounds prohibited by law.

Most states also have fair housing laws on their books, as do many local jurisdictions. These state and local fair housing laws and ordinances may go beyond the federal Fair Housing Law to prohibit discrimination based on physical or mental disabilities, marital status, or age, to name a few.

Overwhelmingly, however, state fair housing laws specifically exempt owner-occupied dwellings from at least some of the provisions. For your interest, I've included in the appendix a chart listing the types of discrimination prohibited by state as well as a listing of states which exempt owner-occupied dwellings from fair housing provisions. It's best to check with the fair housing offices in your locality, however, to find out what state and local laws may apply to you.

Even though some states and localities do not have exemptions for homeowners, I have been unable to find any fair housing lawsuits brought against an owner because he or she turned down an applicant who wanted to share the owner's house.

It is unlikely that any court would ever force you to live with someone in your own house with whom you feel uncomfortable, for whatever personal reasons you may have. That said, it is important to remember that blacks, Hispanics, the handicapped, and people from foreign countries have historically faced discrimination in housing in this country. Further, it was not so long ago that you couldn't

14

buy or rent a house in certain locations if you were Catholic, or Jewish, or Asian-American, or an "Oakie," or a single female, or . . .

My own advice is try to imagine what it would feel like if you were the one being discriminated against, and then put stereotypes aside. The most important question to ask yourself about a prospective tenant is, "Do I feel comfortable with this individual?" If you do, fine. If you don't feel comfortable, don't rent to that person. Never rent to someone just because you want to help someone out. You are not running a social service agency. Evaluate each prospective tenant on his or her personal merits.

Where to Find Tenants

After you have decided what category of tenant you want and what characteristics you would prefer the tenant to have, you can then create an advertising strategy to find a renter. What kind of a person do you want? A woman between the ages of 25 to 30 who is a nonsmoker? a vegetarian? a medical student? a person who is retired?

An excellent place to start looking for tenants is through your own network of friends or neighbors.

You may also post notices at

- Work
- Churches, synagogues, or mosques
- Colleges and universities
- Libraries
- Ethnic or vegetarian restaurants
- Bookstores
- Health food stores
- Military bases
- Apartment complexes—particularly those being converted to condominiums

If you are looking for a tenant who meets unusual criteria, you may want to target your advertising to a specialized audience. For someone who keeps kosher, try synagogue bulletin boards, Jewish newspapers, kosher restaurants, and Hebrew bookstores. Looking for an older person who is also a vegetarian? Try senior citizen organizations, vegetarian restaurants, health food stores, and apartment complexes which have a large percentage of senior citizens among the residents.

If your requirements are less specialized, I believe you will get your best response by putting an ad in the classified section of the largest newspaper in your locality or one that carries a lot of advertisements for housesharing. Run your ad on the weekend. That's when most people have time to look.

What to Put in an Advertisement

Everyone knows that the purpose of an advertisement is to have interested people call you. When you stop to think about it, though, a good advertisement should also be designed to help you screen out people who would not make suitable tenants.

If you are looking for someone who is about 35 years old and is willing to pay $250 per month in rent, there is no need to waste the time of an 18-year-old who can only afford to pay $125 per month. That's why it's important to make your advertisement as clear as possible, specifying:

- What type of person you want
- How much an applicant should be willing to pay
- What kind of accommodations you have to offer

As a first step, I would study the layout of the classified section. Each newspaper has different categories. You need to decide where you will place your ad—under "Rooms, Houses, Apts. to Share"? "Unfurnished Apts."? "Furnished Rooms"? "Sublets"? "Roommates"?

Then scrutinize the wording of the advertisements under that classified section in which you'll place your own ad, and ask yourself which advertisements you think are well-written.

Here are some ads for housemates which I think are clear and provide a lot of information:

> Kensington. M vegetarian, 30, to shr house w same, 25–35. Washer/dryer, fireplace. $275+ 123-4567.

> Brookline. F senior citizen to shr 2 bdrm lux apt w same. Priv bath. $425 includes utilities. 234-5678.

> Burbank. 1 bdrm avail in 4 bdrm co-ed hse nr college. F 21–25 preferred. Pets ok. $195+ ¼ utils. 910-1112.

An ad for a boarder might look like this:

> Bowie. Furn rm w bath. Kit priv. Prefer employed gentleman, nonsmoker. References recqd. $60/wk. 678-9101.

In each case, someone reading one of the above advertisements would know the general location of the house, some of the attractive features of the place, how much rent was being asked, what type of person the occupant was looking for, and, in the ads for housemates, some of the characteristics of the person or people already in the house.

You may have to advertise an accessory dwelling unit a little differently if you place your advertisement in the "apartment" section of the classifieds. Public newspapers are prohibited by fair housing laws from discriminatory advertising. Although for housemates most newspapers will permit you to state a sex preference or age-range preference, and some will even permit you to state racial or religious preferences, you will not be able to do so in advertisements placed in the "apartment" category.

So, an ad for an ADU might read:

> Georgetown. 1 bdrm bsmt apt in twnhse. Priv entrance, own kitchen, fireplace, w/d, patio. $650. 234-5678.

Examples of Ads Which Are Not Clear

Examples of ads that are missing important information follow. See if you can find the problems.

> Waltham. Responsible person to shr nice 6 bdrm
> house. Call Pat at 123-4567.

If you were looking for a place to rent, you would not know from reading this ad:

1. What the rent is
2. If Pat is a man or a woman
3. How many people will be living in the house

> Woman will shr Pepper Pike home w nonsmoker.
> CAC, W/D, DW, WWC, HBO, yd. Nr. I-271. $250 total.
> 345-6789

The main problem with this ad is that few people will completely understand all the abbreviations. The translation of the abbreviations in the first and second lines is "central air conditioning, washer/dryer, dishwasher, wall-to-wall carpeting, home box office, and yard." In addition, it would appear that the owner does not care about the sex or the age of a potential tenant, seeing they are not specified. If the woman really wanted to share her house with someone of the same sex and a similar age but forgot to include these characteristics, she may waste a considerable amount of time fielding phone calls from people who might not be suitable.

Special Advertising Rates

When you phone the newspaper to place your ad, find out if there are special rates. Some newspapers substantially reduce their rates if you place a three-line ad for 3 days or a two-line advertisement for a week. Try to shorten your advertisement to fit the newspaper's special rate guidelines. However, don't overabbreviate to the point that most people won't know what you are talking about.

How to Design a Notice

You have more space to describe your rental when you design a notice for a bulletin board.

Type or neatly print your notices on brightly colored paper to attract someone passing by the bulletin board. Then put them in the strategic locations you have selected.

Here's an example of a short notice with a lot of information:

HOUSE TO SHARE   5/2

Clifton, Gaslight Area. Female, 28, with one 3-year-old child
   is looking for a male/female 25–40 to share elegant,
   renovated house with us. Person would have his or her own
   huge bedroom, which has a skylight, and a private bathroom.
Rent is $375/mo. plus ½ of utilities.
Available June 1.
Please phone after 6:00 P.M. on weekdays or on weekends.
   123-4567

House to Share 123-4567 | House to Share 123-4567 | House to Share 123-4567 | House to Share 123-4567 | House to Share 123-4567 | House to Share 123-4567 | House to Share 123-4567 | House to Share 123-4567

Referral Services

In addition to looking for tenants on your own, you can also try to find them through roommate referral services. There are both public and private roommate referral services around the country. The ones which are publicly funded are usually targeted specifically to match owners of houses with those looking for houses to share. These public programs normally don't get involved matching renters looking for other renters to share houses or apartments. Most of the public programs are also directed toward senior citizens, the handicapped, and lower-income residents.

The advantages to these programs are that screening has, to some extent, been done for you, and the service is often free. The disadvantage is that you often don't have a broad selection of applicants.

The switchboard operator at your local government office should be able to tell you if your community has such a program, or at least connect you with an office which would have that information.

Private roommate referral services, on the other hand, serve a different segment of the population. Most of their clientele are in their midtwenties to late thirties and are affluent enough to be able to pay the agency a fee.

A private roommate referral service may get a fee either from the person looking for a place to rent or from the occupant of the house or apartment who is looking for a housemate, or, often, from both parties.

You can find private roommate referral services in the Yellow Pages or in the classified section of your newspaper.

Whether or not you go through a private or a public roommate referral service, you will be asked to complete a questionnaire asking about your house, rental terms, and personal preferences as to the type of tenant you want. Then the agency will screen its applicants and send you one or more people. You would make the selection, negotiate the rental terms, and perform your own credit check.

Occasionally, real estate agents may help you select a tenant for a house you plan to share. A real estate agent may actually screen a tenant for you, negotiate a lease agreement, and perform a credit check on applicants. The commission for this complete service varies, but it may run anywhere from one-half month's rent to a full month's rent.

The quality of these different kinds of roommate-finding services is uneven. The best ones do the most prescreening. Some will even visit your home so they can give an accurate description to potential tenants.

You may want to check the reputation of a roommate referral service before using it. Ask the agency if it can give you the names and phone numbers of several clients. Your local Better Business Bureau would also know if any complaints were lodged against the agency you plan to use.

What to Say to Callers

Your notices and advertisements should bring you phone calls. So will your registering with a referral service. You will be able to do much of your screening by telephone.

The Tenant

When someone calls regarding my ad, I immediately ask them if they have specific questions or if they would prefer to hear my "running monologue." Most callers will chuckle, and nine out of ten callers ask you to proceed with your monologue. Before I do, though, I say, "Before I tell you about the place, may I ask you a couple of quick questions?" These questions will let me know immediately if the caller stands any chance of being a prospective tenant:

"How old are you?"

"Are you a smoker or a nonsmoker?"

"Do you have a pet, and if so, what kind?"

"Are you looking just for yourself?"

"If you find a place you like, how long would you intend to stay?"

I have chosen the above questions because they require only short, objective answers. One wrong answer will eliminate a caller, so I don't have to waste time going through my entire spiel.

You will be amazed to discover that even if you advertise for one person who is 28–38, an occasional 17-year-old may phone who wants to move in with her boyfriend. Or even though you've specified you want a nonsmoker, someone will phone who "just smokes four or five cigarettes a day at home."

I have some inflexible criteria for screening callers. I definitely want a female, nonsmoker, who is 25 or older and has no pets other than a goldfish or a parakeet. I also want someone who is committed to staying at my house a minimum of 6 months.

If the caller's answers are satisfactory, I then proceed to tell callers more about the house, about myself, and about the terms of the rental.

You may want to start off by giving callers a more precise location of the house, as this is usually a primary concern of most people who will be phoning. Don't give them your exact address, though, just identify the nearest major cross streets or the house location in relation to a major landmark. There is no need to let anyone know exactly where you live until you decide that the caller is someone who is a reasonably good prospect.

Describe the attractive features of the house, and be objective about the less desirable features. For example, mention the skylights, the wall-to-wall carpeting, and the fact that the subway is only two blocks away. However, you may also want to let callers know that the bedroom available does not have a large closet.

It's important to be honest. For one thing, the caller will appreciate it, and it's helpful to establish a trusting, open, friendly relationship from the beginning. Besides, the caller may have a large wardrobe, and if the closet space is minimal, why waste your time and the caller's time by showing the room?

Next, tell the people who phone a little about yourself, and if you have another person in the household, describe that other person as well. You may want to mention your age and what you do for a living. Describe your lifestyle too. Are you quiet or do you entertain a lot? Do you have pets? Do you have an immaculate house or are you more relaxed about housekeeping? Let the caller know.

Conclude your "running monologue" by describing the terms of the rental agreement.* Is there a month-to-month agreement? Do you expect someone to stay a minimum of 6 months? Will a tenant be expected to pay a security deposit, and if so, how much? Let callers know if they will be paying a share of the utility bills and how much you estimate that amount will be on the average per month.

Let callers know what your expectations are, and explain why you have these expectations. So, for example, you may say, "Although there is only a month-to-month written agreement, we are really look-ing for someone who will stay a minimum of 6 months. I like to have a pretty stable household. I require the first and last month's rent plus a $150 security deposit. It's a lot of money, I know, but it's the only way to ensure that I'll get 30 days' notice when someone leaves and have enough left over to cover a tenant's share of the utility bills after he or she leaves."

At the end of my description of the house, the terms of the rental, and my own lifestyle, I let callers know what day I'm planning to show the house. I explain that no one should feel that he or she has to be the first appointment of the day, because I'll be meeting all prospective tenants before making a decision. I tell callers I would appreciate their letting me know, after seeing the place, if they decide they are *not* interested. On the other hand, they should also let me know if they think they might be interested in renting from me. If

* See the rental agreement in Chapter 3.

callers show any interest, I'll phone them back at the end of the weekend to let them know who has been selected.

By the time you have finished your so-called monologue you will have a pretty good sense if the caller is a serious applicant. Callers will usually eliminate themselves during the course of your explanation. Your request for a security deposit, for example, will stop the conversation right away for some callers who can't come up with the money. Others will let you know in no uncertain terms that they could never live with someone so uptight that they wash their dishes every day. Still others may be allergic to your cat. It is just as well that these callers screen themselves out as soon as possible.

It is a very positive sign if the caller chuckles at some of your comments you hope are "cute." Not only does it show that he or she has an excellent sense of humor by appreciating your clever comments—not only does it bolster your ego—but what is more important, really, is that it shows that the person on the other end of the line has a sense of warmth and empathy, two qualities that can't be objectively measured, but which are so important when you are living with others.

After you have finished, ask callers if they have any additional questions that haven't been answered. Answer all the questions as honestly as possible. Then it's your turn. Ask the callers about themselves.

You may want to ask questions related to the caller's

- Type of work
- Length of time at same job
- Length of time in the area
- Leisure activities
- Length of time in current residence
- Reason for wanting to leave current residence

The reason for asking some questions is to find out if you feel that the caller will be compatible with you. Frankly, you could even ask someone a question about the weather and get a positive or negative reaction to the person, indicating if you will get along or not. However, it's easier to identify your feelings by asking more personal questions, like, "What do you do in your spare time?" "Why are you leaving the place you're living in now?" or "What are you looking for in a housemate?"

Beyond the feeling of compatibility, your questions will help you objectively assess if the individual has a stable lifestyle. For me this means that the caller has to have lived in one place and worked at the same job for at least 1 year within the last 2 or 3 years.

Stability counts for a lot with me. Ordinarily I wouldn't take in a housemate who didn't have a job, but I've even done that on occasion. One housemate was a French woman who had just spent 6 years in Senegal. She was unemployed when she came to me and had no permit to work in this country. However, she had worked for the same firm for 5 years in Senegal, and she had enough money in her bank account to pay rent for at least 6 months. I accepted her as a tenant. Within a month she got a job in an embassy. (People who work for embassies don't need U.S. work permits.) Stephanie stayed with me beyond the requisite amount of time, always paid her rent and her bills promptly, and was certainly one of the most interesting housemates I've had.

Ability to pay the required rent and security deposit is just as important as stability. However, you usually don't have to bother to ask if a person can afford it. When you mention your requirement—getting the first and last month's rent plus deposit before someone moves in—during your "running monologue," callers who can't pay will usually find some excuse to give why they aren't interested in making an appointment to see the house.

To sum up, what I mainly want are indications that someone

- Has a lifestyle compatible with my own
- Has a pattern of living characterized by *stability*
- Is able and willing to meet my requirements for first and last month's rent plus the security deposit

Red Flags—Proceed with Caution

In my book *Managing Your Rental House for Increased Income*, I listed eight kinds of callers to be wary of when screening applicants for a rental house. The same rules apply if you're screening someone to share your own house. Here they are:

24

The Person Who Wants to Move In Immediately

Beware of the caller who is in a hurry to move into your house. Usually, the only exception here would be someone who has just come into town and is staying in a hotel.

Most people have to give 30 days' notice before leaving their current residence. If they are prepared to move at a moment's notice, it could mean:

- They are being or have been evicted.
- They are having serious problems with the person or people with whom they are currently living.
- They are impulsive by nature, and they may impulsively decide to move out of your house on the spur of the moment too.

The Person Who Demands to Know Your Address and Wants to Come Over Immediately

Although many callers ask for a more specific location of the house, only a few will start off the conversation by asking for an address and say they want to come over immediately. There is an air of desperation in such a request. Good potential tenants will want to ask you questions about the house and the rental terms before deciding if they want to look at the house.

The Person Who Has Moved Frequently and/or Changed Jobs Frequently

Be careful of the person who has had more than two jobs or more than two places of residence within the past year. Often, such a person has some personality problems or economic difficulties.

The Person Who Argues about Your Deposit Requirements

If you explain the reasons why you need to get the first month's rent, the last month's rent, and a security deposit, and the caller responds that he or she sees no reason for this because "I am a trustworthy person," I immediately conclude that the caller is not a trustworthy person. Thereupon I simply explain that I understand that I'm asking for a lot of money. Nonetheless, it's a requirement for all of my tenants. I thank the person for calling, explain that I'm sorry it won't work out, and say good-bye. *The person who argues about the deposit will be the first person to damage the house and try to move out without notice.* Good tenants will understand why you need the security deposit.

The Person Who Is Currently Living with Friends or Family

If someone is currently living with friends or family, find out why and how long they have been in that situation. Sometimes people who have just been evicted or have just come out of a mental health or a correctional facility have no other place to go but family or friends. Their backgrounds may or may not exclude them from being your tenant, but you should be aware of any potential problems.

The Person Who Works at Home or Is In Between Jobs

I have, on rare occasions, taken in a tenant who was unemployed. Usually, though, it behooves you to look for someone who is a full-time worker or a full-time student. Your tenants should work or study outside of the house. Tenants should not be permitted to conduct business from your house. Not only may such an arrangement violate zoning codes, but you may feel uncomfortable if your home is turned into a place of business.

The Person Who Objects to the Personal Questions You Ask

I quickly terminate the conversation with a person who objects to my personal questions by saying, "I have a feeling that this isn't going to work out."

There must be honesty and open communication between owner and tenant from the start. It is imperative to get a housing and employment history, and sometimes to get more personal information if, from the conversation, you sense that the person doesn't expect to share household chores or plans to have a boyfriend or a girlfriend practically move in as well.

The person who is offended by your questions will not make a good tenant.

The Person Who Owns a Junky Car

Watch out for applicants who drive up in junky cars. I don't mean old cars; I mean cars with smashed headlights, badly dented doors, torn seats, and an accumulation of trash scattered on the floor. It is almost a guarantee that a tenant who keeps a junky car will keep his or her room the same way.

How to Handle an Obscene Phone Caller

There is one last group of callers who are interested in talking with you about matters completely unrelated to your ad—the obscene phone callers. You will probably get at least one obscene phone call if your ad indicates that you are female.

At first such calls used to terrorize me. Now I am occasionally exasperated by them, sometimes amused by them, but mainly bored by them.

As soon as the nature of the call becomes apparent, do not hang up. Don't fight the caller. Don't say a word. Don't blow a whistle in his ear. Simply put the phone down off the receiver and walk away. When the caller realizes nobody is listening to him, he will hang up. If he phones again, do the same thing. The obscene caller only gets his kicks if you act scared, or hang up in a panic, or talk to him. Don't react in any way, and the caller will hang up and not bother you again.

Telephone Answering Machines

Telephone answering machines are a blessing! If you can possibly afford it, I suggest that you buy one. Otherwise, you're going to feel trapped in the house waiting for the phone to ring. Every time you go out to buy groceries or to run an errand, you will worry that you are missing phone calls from potential tenants.

You will be able to return phone calls at your convenience if you have an answering machine, and you'll already know useful information like the caller's name, home phone number, and office number.

I suggest that you keep your outgoing message short and to the point. My message goes like this:

"Hello, and thanks for calling. This is Doreen. Please don't hang up. If you phoned about the ad for a house to share, the place is still available. I want to talk with you, but I can't come to the phone right now. At the sound of the tone, please leave your name and number, both at home and at work, and I'll get back to you just as soon as I can. Wait for the beep and leave your message. Thank you."

Keeping Track of Callers

You need to have an organized list of the people who phone about your rental.

Initially I wrote down the names of the people who phoned on any piece of scrap paper available at the phone I happened to be using. Then I had a hard time remembering who was supposed to come at what time to look at the house. Sometimes I accidentally scheduled two people at the same time or forgot when someone was supposed to show up.

Scheduling becomes much easier if you always use the same phone in the house when speaking with prospective tenants. At that phone, have a sheet of paper divided into the following columns:

- Date
- Person's Name
- Home Telephone Number
- Office Telephone Number
- Comments
- Appointment

Make sure you record all your calls on that one list. Here's an example of a "List of Callers":

LIST OF CALLERS

Date	Person's Name	Home Tel.	Office Tel.	Comments	Appt.
3/29	Arlene Allen	123-4567	891-0111	26; Secretary at Ace Marketing for 2 yrs; 3yrs. in current apt.; apt. going condo	Sat. 2 PM
3/29	Betty Boop	121-3145		18; wants job as model; currently unemployed	No
3/29	Carol Clairol	161-7189	202-1222	27; membership director for League of Hairdressers for 1 yr; separating from husband; owned condo for 2 years	Sat. 3 PM
3/29	Deborah Daring	242-5262	282-9303	25; reporter at Star for 9 mo.; former Peace Corps volunteer for 2 yrs. in Gambia; may work unusual hrs.; lived in same apt. for 1 yr.	Sat. 2:30 PM

29

You should find the "List of Callers" to be helpful throughout the screening process.

1. You can use the list to refresh your memory about the caller before the scheduled appointment.

2. If your plans change or you need to confirm an appointment, you'll easily be able to figure out whom you need to phone.

3. You may want to phone to find out why someone, who said he or she was coming, failed to keep the appointment.

4. After you have chosen a tenant, you'll have a complete list of names to let applicants know of your decision, one way or another.

How to Schedule Appointments with Callers

It's important not to crowd your schedule. You will want to be able to spend time with each person individually so you can get to know each other better.

After you have screened a caller over the telephone, and have determined that the person may make a suitable tenant, make an appointment for the individual to see the house and to meet you. I try to schedule most of my appointments on a Sunday afternoon, allowing at least a half hour for each person coming by. After all, you may be doing business with each other for a year or two, or even longer.

There are several reasons to try to schedule all appointments in one afternoon.

- It saves you time because you don't have to tie up several evenings or afternoons waiting for people to look at your house.

- You will see several people within a short period of time, so you can compare one to the other more easily because your memory of each will be fresh.

- You can make a decision that day; whereas if you had different appointments scattered throughout the week, you might have to withhold a decision for several days until you had seen the last caller. In the meantime, your first choice may have found other accommodations.

How to Reduce the Number of People Who Don't Show Up for an Appointment

One of the minor aggravations in life is waiting in vain for some people to keep their appointments.

Be resigned to the fact that a few of your appointments are just not going to show up. It's one of the frustrations of this business.

You can reduce the number of times people cancel their appointments without telling you if, after you schedule someone to see the house, you say, "May I ask you for a favor?" The caller will respond, "Sure." Then you say, "If for any reason you decide you can't make it, would you mind phoning to let me know?" Once you get a verbal commitment, usually people will let you know if they won't be able to make it.

Meeting Your Callers in Person

Review your "List of Callers" and refresh your memory about your caller before the person shows up for the appointment so you can greet the potential tenant by name at the door and ask more intelligent questions when you start to get to know each other. Show each person the whole house if you are looking for a housemate. If you plan to rent to a boarder or to someone living in an accessory dwelling unit, you may just want to show callers their quarters and the areas of the house they will be entitled to use. Point out convenient features and answer any questions they may have.

Saying "Yes"

If you like the person and think he or she would make a responsible tenant, sit down after the tour of the house to have a chat. You may want to start off a conversation by asking what the caller thinks of the house in comparison to other places he or she has seen. If someone obviously likes the place a lot, you may then want to ask, "What type of characteristics do you feel are important in others if you will be sharing a house together?" Now is the time to talk about lifestyles. You may want to discuss the house rules regarding alcohol, drugs, boyfriends or girlfriends staying overnight, out-of-town guests, and housekeeping chores. Make sure that your expectations are compatible with the applicant's.

As a general rule I suggest that you do not make a decision or force the prospective tenant to make a decision on the spot. Both of you should have time to think it over. You may want to let exceptionally good prospects know that you like them and that as far as you are concerned, you think things would work out pretty well. Nonetheless, you have promised others that you would not rent on a first-come, first-served basis and that you have a few other appointments lined up. Ask good prospects if they would mind if you phoned them back at a certain time—say, the following evening at 6:00 P.M. to let them know your decision.

Saying "No"

It is very difficult for me, and I suspect for most people, to have to reject applicants. Fortunately, in most cases you won't have to. If you are uncomfortable with some potential renters, the chances are good that they aren't comfortable with you either.

But what do you do if an individual wants to rent from you and you just don't feel comfortable with that person? If you have followed the suggestions in this book, you can legitimately tell the individual that you promised all callers that the vacancy would not be filled on a first-come, first-served basis. You have other people to see before you make your decision. If you are lucky, you'll find someone else that day to rent the place.

When you phone back applicants who were not accepted, let them know you appreciated meeting them, but someone else was selected. Rarely will someone you have rejected ask why.

It is more difficult to turn down someone if you still haven't been able to fill your vacancy. You can, of course, always say that you want to see more people before making a decision, and it may take you several weeks before you select someone.

I think, though, that it is a lot kinder to let a person know as soon as possible that he or she will not be selected. The problem is to phrase your rejection in a way that will hurt the least.

First, I try to think of reasons which have nothing to do with the individual's personality. Perhaps the person works a night shift, and you feel that the odd hours will bother you. Or perhaps you feel that the applicant would bring too much furniture into the house.

If I can't think of some objective reason to turn down an applicant, I'll say something like this:

"I have been thinking a lot about you. You seem like a nice person. I don't know why, though, but I sense that if you moved in I'm not sure it would work out. I can't explain it. I thought about putting you off by telling you I hadn't made a decision yet, but I thought you'd appreciate honesty more."

What to Do If You Are Unable to Rent Your Place Immediately

Don't panic if you can't find a suitable tenant right away. One time it took me seven weekends of advertising before I found an acceptable housemate.

After advertising unsuccessfully for a few weeks, though, you may want to assess your situation. Are the room or rooms you plan to rent out as attractive as possible? Is your ad worded well? Is your rent appropriate? Curiously, I have sometimes found I got a better response to my ad by raising the rent rather than lowering it. As mentioned previously some higher-caliber tenants will not respond to an ad which has too low a rent, because they think the place must be a dump.

The most useful information you get will be from callers who come to look at the place. You may want to ask them how your place compares with other places they have seen, and if the rent you are asking is in the fair range. You will usually get very honest answers to your questions.

The Importance of Tenant Selection

The most crucial part of the rental process is tenant selection. You don't have to feel that you are selecting a tenant who will become your best friend, but you do have to feel comfortable with the person you select. If there is *any* question in your mind that you might not be able to get along with a prospective tenant, *do not agree to*

33

rent to that person. If you have just bought a house and a large mortgage payment is due, there is a great temptation to think, "I'll take anyone who can pay the rent." Never give in to that temptation!

Selecting a tenant is somewhat akin, in greatly modified form, to selecting a spouse. *As my father once told me, "Before you get married, keep both eyes wide open. After you get married, keep one eye half shut."* In a nutshell, this philosophy can be applied to selecting and keeping compatible tenants.

Points to Remember

1. Determine if you want a housemate, boarder, or a tenant, and decide what personal characteristics are important to you.

2. Implement an advertising strategy which may include contacting your network of friends, posting notices in public places, listing your rental with the housing offices of organizations, and placing ads in newspapers.

3. Write notices and ads which will let people know about (1) the house, (2) some characteristics of the person(s) with whom they would share the house, and (3) the terms of the rental.

4. Make a list of the names and phone numbers of callers, and jot down impressions of them when you talk with them.

5. Screen callers carefully on the phone, making an appointment only with the most promising.

6. Schedule appointments at intervals of one half hour or longer so you can give undivided attention to each prospective tenant.

7. "Before selecting a tenant, keep both eyes wide open. After a tenant has moved in, keep one eye half shut." *See next chapter on management.*

3

THE MANAGEMENT

How an Applicant Becomes a Tenant

An applicant officially becomes your tenant when you and that person sign a lease or rental agreement. With very few exceptions, the agreement should be sealed with a check from the tenant for the required rent and deposit.

Before you accept an applicant as your tenant, though, it is a very good idea to check references. In all honesty, I don't always check references for the people I select as tenants. I tend to trust my instincts, after ten years of selecting housemates. Nonetheless, I strongly suggest that you do as I say—"check references"—not as I do, at least until you are very comfortable with the whole process of tenant selection. You have nothing to lose by making a few phone calls, and the simple task of checking references may save you from future aggravation.

How to Check References

One way to proceed is to have all people, who look at your house and who show an interest in moving in, fill out a rental application, similar to the one you see below. You can review the applications at your leisure when everyone has left. Then phone the person you

TENANT APPLICATION FORM

1. Name of Prospective Tenant *Marie-Jo Land*
2. Home No. *109-8765* Office No. *432-1012 X 41*
3. Present Occupation *Lab Technician*
4. Name and Address of Firm *Smathers Laboratory*
   5962 S. Chelm Street
   Mainville
5. Name of Supervisor *Lois Lewis*
   Telephone Number of Supervisor *432-1012 X43*
6. Previous Occupation (if employed less than 6 months at present job *NA*
7. Name of Previous Supervisor *NA*
   Telephone No. of Previous Supervisor _____
8. Address(es) of Applicant for Last 2 Years

Address	Dates	Landlord	Telephone No.
2619 N. Gomel St. #12 Mainville	6/84 – 7/86	Michael Flott	201-9181

9. Name, Address, and Phone Number of Nearest Relative

   DON & Marie   *150 W. 96th St.*
   Land (Parents)   *N.Y., NY 10201*   *(212) 123-4567*
   Name _____ Address _____ Phone

10. Name and Phone Number of Two Friends Locally

   Jay Cutler *891-2345*   *Karin Sparrow* *891-5432*
   Name Phone Name Phone

COMMENTS:

Supervisor says that Marie-Jo is a very dependable worker and has an excellent record.
Landlord says she usually paid her rent on time except for one month when she explained she would be late; he would rent to her again if she were looking for a place.

have selected. If the applicant agrees to become your tenant, explain that you just need to check the references on the application before he or she can come over to sign the rental agreement.

Or you may decide *not* to have everyone fill out an application who is interested in renting. Instead, phone the individual whom you have selected, and if the person wants to move in, say you'd be delighted, but you just need to check some references first. Then ask for the names and telephone numbers of the following:

- Current supervisor at work
- Previous supervisor if applicant has worked in current job less than 6 months
- Current landlord
- Previous landlord if applicant has lived in current residence less than 6 months

You may also want to find out the name and phone number of a current or previous housemate to find out how the individual gets along with others.

Here are some questions you can ask the people you phone:

For Employers

- How long have you known the applicant?
- In what capacity have you known the applicant?
- Generally, how would you describe this person as an employee?
- How does he or she seem to get along with the rest of the people at work?

For Landlords/Housemates

- How long have you known the applicant?
- How did he or she keep the place?

- How did this person seem to get along with the rest of the people in the household?
- Did he or she have any difficulty paying the rent on time?
- Do you know why the person is leaving (left)?
- Would you rent to this individual again?

By asking these questions, you are trying to find out:

1. If what the applicant has told you is true
2. How the applicant relates to others
3. If the applicant appears to be conscientious

I know that many other applications are far more detailed than my own. But, frankly, I don't care what someone's car payments are or even how much money someone makes a year. As long as a person has a history of making timely rent payments, getting along reasonably well with others, and taking responsibility seriously, why should I care about other personal details of this individual's life?

Last Steps to Take

It's important to complete the reference check as soon as possible and have a rental agreement signed very quickly thereafter. Until you have a signed rental agreement and a check in hand, you have nothing tangible to show that you indeed have a tenant for your house.

I usually ask the person to come over to my house to complete the rental procedure over a cup of tea. At that time:

- We go over the terms of the rental agreement.
- The person signs two copies of the rental agreement—one is for me; the other is for the tenant to keep.
- He or she hands over a check for the first month's rent, the last month's rent, and the security deposit.
- I hand over a key to the house.
- We discuss plans for moving in.

Incidentally, I also have tenants fill out a rental application when they come over to the house to sign the rental agreement if they haven't filled one out previously. The information on the form can be useful, even if you are not going to check references. For example, in an emergency, you may need to contact the tenant's nearest relative or reach your tenant at work.

A General Philosophy of Management

I have four general principles of management. You already know the first:

"Keep One Eye Half Shut"

Don't let every little petty annoyance bother you. Whenever you live with someone else—whether that person is a parent, a spouse, or a child—it is likely that he or she is going to do things which bother you at least some of the time. In turn, you may exhibit some behavior which they may not find agreeable. Although you and your tenant should be able to approach each other with your concerns, generally speaking, both of you will be happier if you "keep one eye half shut" about most of the habits of the other.

My other three management principles are:

Tenants are your customers.

Assault problems, not tenants.

Create and abide by fair rules.

Tenants Are Your Customers

There is a common misconception that an owner must show tenants who is "boss" or they will take advantage of the owner. In reality, tenants are more like your customers. It is in both your interests if tenants are satisfied with the product and services you are providing.

In addition, your tenants may be your friends. However, if you are to maintain a profitable enterprise, your tenants should realize that there is a business aspect to your personal relationship, and no matter how much you like them, the business aspect will come first.

To me this means that if, for example, a tenant loses her job and tells me she can't pay the rent, I respond sympathetically to her plight, and let her know how much I'll miss having her as a tenant. This may sound "cold," but keep in mind that your tenant has parents, brothers, sisters, and friends who might be able to help out. If you miss that rent, there could be an additional $200 or more coming out of your own pocket each month when it comes time to pay the mortgage. I'm not prepared to subsidize a tenant to that extent.

Assault Problems, Not Tenants

Inevitably, some problems will arise in a household which either can't be or won't be ignored. You, as the owner, are responsible for "keeping cool" and setting the stage for finding a solution to the problem.

You, your tenant, and a problem are three. If you and your tenant are on the same side, you will easily overcome the problem. If you and your tenant do not cooperate, the problem will hurt both of you in turn.

It is rarely helpful to assault a person verbally. It is very helpful to assault a problem with the help of your tenant. Some of the most common household problems and possible solutions are discussed later in this chapter.

Create and Abide by Fair Rules

Day-to-day behavior by owners and tenants flows naturally in a household, without conscious thought of written or verbal agreements, if you have picked a compatible tenant. However, the underlying basis of a harmonious household is for the owner and tenant alike to be aware that both have agreed to abide by a fair set of rules, both written and unwritten.

The Advantages of Using a Written Agreement

Some owners don't bother to have written agreements with tenants who share their houses. They feel that verbal agreements will suffice, and writing down the terms of the rental just seems too formal and stuffy.

I would agree that verbal commitments and understandings are very important. A verbal commitment might not be *legally* binding, but if you have chosen your tenants well, they will feel some *moral* obligation to carry out their verbal promises.

Written rental agreements are essential, too, though in addition to any verbal understandings. A well-written agreement will define the basic rights and responsibilities of the owner and the tenant, protecting each. If a dispute arises, a written agreement can usually settle the issue, provided that both parties are well-intentioned.

Without a written agreement, it is possible for even two well-meaning people to disagree on a point. For example, a tenant may pay a security deposit, and after 2 years, the tenant remembers having paid a $250 deposit, while the owner is sure it was only $200.

It's, therefore, important to write down all major terms of the rental. The question is how detailed you want the agreement to be.

Now some owners only feel secure if absolutely every last detail is in writing. I have seen single-spaced leases that run for three pages on both sides of legal-sized paper.

I would not recommend such a detailed rental agreement. The truth is that it is highly unlikely that you and your tenant are ever going to contest the terms of the agreement in a courtroom. The written agreement is only as good as the intentions and word of the people who sign it.

Instead, I'd opt for clarity and simplicity in an agreement between people who live in the same household. You should be able to talk with your tenant about any unusual occurrences outside the scope of the rental agreement and achieve a verbal understanding about what will be done.

How to Write Your Own Rental Agreement

Before you write up a rental agreement, you first need to decide if you want to have a lease with your tenant. A lease is a rental agreement made for a predetermined length of time—often for a year.

If a rental agreement is open-ended, it is not officially called a lease. A rental agreement which is not a lease may be on a week-to-week basis or, more commonly, on a month-to-month basis. It has no fixed day of termination and no fixed terms of the rental beyond that one-week or one-month period of time.

If you have a month-to-month agreement, for example, you could choose to raise the rent of your tenant every month, with 30 days' notice; or ask a tenant to leave for no particular reason, with 30 days of notice. The tenant is not bound beyond a 30-day period, either, and a tenant you thought would stay for a year may suddenly announce that he or she is leaving after staying a month in your house.

I usually recommend that owners have month-to-month agreements, rather than leases, with the tenants with whom they are sharing their homes, despite certain drawbacks to this arrangement. The main reason I favor month-to-month agreements is because if the tenancy is not working out, both you and your tenant should be in a position to terminate the agreement as quickly as possible. There should be no obligation for either party to stick it out another 9 months to finish some lease.

I don't use month-to-month agreements in order to raise the rent frequently—that's not an issue. Your tenants would probably leave you if you tried to do that anyway. But month-to-month agreements have these other advantages as well:

- They usually can be less complicated than leases because you do not have to put in all the contingencies which may occur in a year's time.

- Month-to-month agreements exert pressure on owners and tenants to be more polite to each other because both parties know that each can terminate the rental agreement with a month's notice if pushed too far.

- Month-to-month agreements are often more attractive to single tenants who might not know what their plans will be in 10 months.

For owners, the only advantage a lease has over a rental agreement is that it seems to guarantee them a tenant for at least a year. However, a lease can't even assure you that your tenant will complete the term of the lease. Let's say your tenant marries or has to move because of a job transfer.

All things considered, I'd opt for month-to-month agreements.

What to Include in Your Rental Agreement

Although you will need to tailor your agreement to fit your particular circumstances, all agreements should contain the following information:

- The names and signatures of the owner and the tenant
- The address of the house in which the tenant is renting a room or rooms
- The term, or length of time, the tenant is committed to staying, including the day tenancy will begin
- The amount of rent to be paid
- When rent will be paid
- The amount of the security deposit, if any

Before you draw up your rental agreement, you will have to do a little research on your state laws. Most states have some kind of residential landlord and tenant act which may regulate:

- How much you can require for a security deposit
- How much interest, if any, you have to pay on a tenant's deposit
- How soon you have to return the deposit after a tenant leaves
- Under what circumstances an owner can deduct money from a tenant's deposit
- How many days' notice an owner must give to a tenant to terminate a tenancy

It's usually not too hard to find out the rental rules in your state and locality. Just phone your local government office and explain that you need to find out the laws regarding residential rentals; or ask which office handles landlord-tenant questions. The switchboard operator should be able to connect you with the right office. Sometimes it's a housing section; other times it's a consumer affairs office or a landlord-tenant commission.

When you find the right office, in addition to asking your questions, find out if the office has any literature on rentals. Many offices have free handbooks clarifying laws pertaining to landlord and tenant relationships in your state.

You may also want to look at copies of other leases and rental agreements, so you can include clauses you think are important in your own agreement. You can find standard rental agreements in:

- Stationery stores
- Real estate offices
- The office which handles landlord-tenant relations in your local government
- Apartment owners' associations

I have included here a slightly modified copy of the agreement I use with my housemates and have inserted circled numbers by points that will be discussed more fully later on. The agreement was designed to be in compliance with Virginia law.

RENTAL AGREEMENT

This agreement has been entered into on *Feb. 12, 1987*, by and between *Bill Parker*_____, hereinafter called Tenant and *Doreen Bierbrier*_____, hereinafter called Owner.

In consideration of a monthly rent of $*245* plus *33.3*% of the utilities ① (specifically for gas, electricity, water, trash collection, and basic telephone service) the Tenant will be entitled to share, on a month-to-month basis, the residence located at *123 Main St., Podunk*_____.

The following are mutually agreed upon points:

② 1. Tenant will begin tenancy on *March 1, 1987*_____.

2. Rent will be due on the *1st* day of every month.

③ 3. Tenant will pay the first month's rent and an equal sum toward the last month's rent before moving in.

④ 4. Tenant will pay a security deposit of $*150* before moving in. Within *30* days after Tenant's departure if all obligations have been paid in full, and if the premises have been maintained in satisfactory condition, the deposit, together with any interest required by law, will be returned to the Tenant. Any deductions will be itemized in writing and sent to the Tenant.

5. The initial utility bill and the last month's utility bill will be prorated

to coincide with the number of days that the Tenant has agreed to occupy the house (i.e., until the last day of the rental period for that month). Otherwise, no matter how many days the Tenant is away from the house during the course of a month, the Tenant is responsible for **33.3**% of the utility bills.

6. Tenant is not permitted to sublet the premises without the express consent of the Owner.

7. Tenant shall make no alterations, additions, or improvements to the premises without the express consent of the Owner.

8. Owner is responsible for paying for the major maintenance, cleaning, and repair of the furnace, roof, water heater, central air conditioning, gutters and outside plumbing, and repairs to major equipment and appliances when used in the course of their normal and proper usage.

9. Tenant is responsible for keeping plumbing fixtures as clean and safe as condition permits, shall unstop and keep clear all waste pipes which are for the Tenant's exclusive use, and will pay for any loss or damage caused by his or her negligence.

10. Owner shall not be liable to Tenant, unless required by law, for any damage or injury to the Tenant nor to the Tenant's guests, nor for any personal property which is stolen or damaged due to flooding, leaks, malfunction of equipment, structural problems, or for any reason whatever. All persons and personal property on said premises associated with the Tenant will be the sole risk and responsibility of the Tenant.

11. This agreement and the tenancy hereby granted may be terminated at any time by either party hereto by giving to the other party not less than 30 days' prior notice in writing. Terminations initiated by the Tenant must end on the last day of the month.

8 Special Provisions:

Bill Parker
TENANT

Doreen Bierbrien
OWNER

Both parties have read this agreement, agree to its terms, and each has a copy.

---

① Utilities

It is advisable to have your tenant share the utility bills if that person is occupying one-fourth or more of your house and intends to stay for more than 2 months. If a tenant is occupying half the house with you, an equitable split of all the utility bills would be 50 percent for you and 50 percent for your tenant. If you have two housemates, you may want to split the bills at 33.33 percent for each of you.

There are several reasons to have a tenant pay for a portion of the utilities rather than including utility payments in a higher rent.

- When advertising for a tenant, the monthly rent looks lower when it does not include utilities and, thus, is more attractive to a potential tenant.

- Your tenant will take care to shut the windows in the winter and use the air conditioner sparingly in summer when he or she is paying part of the bill.

- If your utility rates go up, you are not forced to raise the rent to cover the increased costs. It is far better for your tenant to be frustrated with the utility companies for their increases than to be frustrated with you because you have increased the rent.

② Date of Tenancy

Sometimes someone you would like as a tenant cannot actually move into the house for several weeks. If this means that you would have a vacancy for awhile, you might want to negotiate with the prospective tenant. You could suggest that you split the time of the vacancy, so that you would lose rent for half that period of time and your tenant would pay rent for half that period of time to ensure the rental.

Tenancy may begin on any day of the month regardless whether the tenant actually moves in that day. That first month, prorate the rent to coincide with the day the tenant agrees to begin tenancy. For example, if the rent is $200 per month and the tenant takes tenancy on the fifteenth of the month, I would calculate the rent for the first month to be $105.28. How is that calculated? What I did was to work out a rent per day by calculating how much rent the tenant would pay in a year and then dividing by 365 days.

$200 × 12 months = $2400 per year
$2400 divided by 365 days = $6.58 per day

Now, assuming the month the tenant moves in has 30 days and the tenant begins occupancy on the fifteenth, she would be occupying the house for 16 days. And 16 days at $6.58 per day is equal to $105.28. No, I didn't make a mistake counting the number of days. There are 16 days until the end of the month if you count the fifteenth as one day. Count the days for yourself.

③ and ④ First and Last Month's Rent and Security Deposit

In a way, points 3 and 4 go together, because these are advance payments you are requiring in order to ensure that your tenant will carry out the terms of the rental agreement. Technically, though, a security deposit is fully refundable if the tenant meets all obligations, so payments of the last month's rent and, of course, the first month's rent are not included as a part of the security deposit.

How much of a security deposit should you require? Well, for a long time my father used to wear suspenders and a belt to make sure nothing was going to fall down. My advice is to make sure you have yourself covered, within the limits of your state laws. Many states limit the amount of the security deposit you can collect.

If the laws of your state permit it, require that the first and last month's rent be paid in advance and, in addition, hold an amount—perhaps 75 percent of a month's rent—as a security deposit. The reason for collecting the last month's rent in advance is to make sure you get 30 days of notice when the tenant decides to leave. Otherwise, a tenant could tell you on the twenty-ninth day of the month that he or she was leaving the next day, and you would have no time to find another tenant before your tenant left.

Notice the phrasing in the agreement, "Tenant will pay the first month's rent and *an equal sum toward the last month's rent* before moving in." The reason I did not say that the tenant will pay the first and last month's rent in advance is to protect you in case of rent increases. Let's say you have a tenant who stays with you for 5 years, and you increase the rent every year. After 5 years, the last month's rent would be higher than the initial deposit the tenant made toward the last month's rent.

The security deposit is loosely termed a "damage deposit." You can use the deposit to cover a tenant's share of unpaid utility

47

bills, phone bills, and any actual damage beyond normal wear and tear.

Security deposits are often the point of contention between owners and tenants. Consumer groups argue that many landlords act as if the money were their own instead of a deposit being held for their tenants. Consumer activists deplore the fact that most states do not even require that a landlord keep the tenant's deposit in an escrow account, separate from an owner's personal funds.

I can understand the position of consumer groups. Some landlords unscrupulously withhold deposits from tenants or squander security deposits which do not rightfully belong to them.

Nonetheless, I don't keep my tenants' deposits in an escrow account or pay interest on them. My house is in a state which only requires owners of 10 or more houses to pay interest on security deposits. There is no requirement for me to open up a separate escrow account for my tenants' deposits, either.

Initially, I did set up a separate account with my tenants' deposits and paid them the interest that accrued even though, legally, I didn't have to. Then I found out that if you pay tenants interest, in addition to taking the time to set up an account, you have to fill out IRS Form 1099 and track down the tenant who may have left, sending that person a copy of the IRS form, while sending another copy to the IRS. All of this for what may have amounted to $5 or $10 per tenant. I now just abide by the letter of the law—no interest on security deposits and no separate account for my tenants.

However you decide to handle security deposits, check on your state laws and make sure the subject is thoroughly discussed with your renter before the rental agreement is signed, to avoid problems later.

In sum, you should know your legal obligations and clearly explain to your tenant:

- Why the deposit is required
- What it could be used to cover
- If interest will be paid on the security deposit, and if so, how much
- When the security deposit will be returned

Any deductions you make from your tenant's security deposit should be itemized. Copies of the bills you have paid with the deposit along with the itemized list of deductions should be enclosed when you return the remainder of the deposit to your former tenant.

⑤ Maintenance and Repairs

As a general rule of thumb, I believe that if a tenant breaks or damages something, either intentionally or not, the tenant should pay to have it fixed. For example, a tenant who jams a garbage disposal by cramming it with celery stalks should have to pay the plumber if you need a professional to fix the disposal.

The owner should pay if damage has occurred which is beyond the tenant's control or if a major appliance or fixture, such as a washer, dryer, refrigerator, air-conditioning unit, furnace, or hot water heater, must be repaired or replaced because of normal wear and tear. If you and your tenant both regularly use small equipment such as toaster-ovens or record players, no matter who owns it, both of you should chip in to pay for repairs if you can't determine who caused the problem.

It is a bit trickier to determine who should pay for plumbing problems. I will fix leaky faucets or corroded plumbing. I will usually assume responsibility for unclogging drains which my tenants and I both use, unless my tenants obviously caused the problem. My tenants, though, are responsible for unclogging plumbing which is for their sole use. This rule makes tenants more cautious about what they flush down the toilet or put in the sink.

⑥ Insurance

Both homeowner and tenant should have insurance. Most homeowners carry a package homeowner's insurance policy. While at least six standardized homeowner's policy forms are used in the United States, Forms HO-2 and HO-3 are the most popular among owner-occupants of houses. Although HO-3 is slightly more comprehensive then HO-2, it does not cover furniture or personal property. Form HO-4 is the insurance used by tenants.

Forms HO-2 and HO-3 cover damages and loss to the house and other structures such as garages. The policy may also protect you against damage caused to the property of others when, for example, your tree falls on your neighbor's car. In addition, this insurance protects the owner from personal liability. For example, if a guest slips on your front porch and sues you for the cost of medical payments, you would be covered. Damage to the owner's personal property may also be covered by Form HO-2, and usually you will be covered against theft, too, *unless your tenant was the culprit.*

Many tenants don't realize that your homeowner's insurance only protects you and your property. Your insurance will not protect your tenant's property from loss or damage, nor will it protect your tenant from personal liability suits, unless the owner's negligence can be proved.

Let's say your tenant stores a stereo in your basement. The basement floods and ruins the stereo. If you had no knowledge that your basement might flood, it is likely that you are not liable for the damage. If, though, you knew that the basement had flooded in the past and you did not reveal this to your tenant, you might well be responsible for any damage which may have occurred to your tenant's property because of the flooding, and your insurance company would have to compensate your tenant for the damage.

On the other hand, let's say that your tenant accidentally causes a grease fire, and your kitchen is destroyed in the fire. Your insurance company might pay for the damage, but then turn around and sue your tenant.

Tenants should consider taking out renter's insurance, Form HO-4, which is similar in coverage to a homeowner's policy, but does not provide coverage for building structures.

Laws and insurance coverage vary from state to state, and may change from time to time. Check with your insurance agent to see whether you need additional coverage if you have tenants in your house.

⑦ Termination

Both owner and tenant have the right to terminate the rental agreement provided proper notice is given. The provision that the tenant's termination date must be the last day of the month is a protection to the owner. It is easier to find another tenant who can move in on the first of the month, minimizing the chance of a vacancy between tenants.

A tenant may move out before the end of the month, even though you have already collected the last month's rent. In this case, try to find another tenant to move into the house as soon as your old tenant moves out. Then prorate the new tenant's rent for those days, and reimburse your former tenant for the days when the other tenant was occupying the rental.

If you can't find a new tenant right away, though, your tenant who is moving before the end of the month is obligated to pay not only for rent until the end of the month but also for a share of the utilities until the last day of legal tenancy (See clause 5 in the Rental Agreement). Outgoing tenants may ask why they have to pay rent and utilities for days in which they are not physically present in the house. My answer is that legally they are entitled to live in the house during that period of time. They have chosen not to. It is a similar situation when people in the household choose to go away on vacation for a couple of weeks. They would still be responsible for paying rent and a share of the utilities even though they were not physically present in the house.

⑧ Special Provisions

Many rental agreements have other provisions including:

- Late charges if the rent is more than 5 days late
- A charge if a rent check bounces
- Prohibitions against pets, or a clause requiring tenants to have the house professionally defleaed and deticked if a pet causes such a problem
- Mandatory tenant insurance

Whatever rental agreement you design, *strive for simplicity, fairness, clarity, and common sense.*

Scheduling Rent Increases

Some owners schedule rent increases in their rental agreements. You don't need to. As I mentioned earlier in the chapter, theoretically, an owner could increase the rent every month if a tenant has a month-to-month agreement, provided that the tenant was given 30 days' notice. Your tenant, however, should be given at least a verbal commitment, before signing the rental agreement, about your policy regarding rent increases.

Your tenant should expect a rent increase on a predictable basis. Think twice before raising the rent for the same tenant more than once a year or on an unplanned basis. If your rent increases are erratic, your tenant may decide to move, and a vacancy may cause you to lose more money than you would gain from your projected rent increase.

My policy is to raise the rent a modest amount for a tenant who has been with me for a year. One reason for raising the rent is because our economy has had a clear overall trend of inflation. Your costs to maintain the household have risen even if your mortgage payments have remained constant. Taxes and insurance increase over time, and repair and maintenance costs have also increased from year to year, even though there is less inflation in some years than in others.

Another reason has simply to do with business. You should strive to charge a fair market value for your rental, keeping pace with what others are charging for similar accommodations.

Normally, though, I save steeper rent increases for the time when a tenant decides to move. A new tenant won't mind paying the higher rent, never having paid the old, lower rent.

Handling Common Household Problems

Your written rental agreement cannot protect you from common household problems which will inevitably arise. The majority of problems which occur in shared households can be minimized if you keep your temper and focus on solving the problem rather than on berating your tenant. The following are five typical situations with suggestions for avoiding problems in the first place or for resolving them if they occur:

Your Tenant Is Not Helping with the Household Chores

- When you screen potential tenants, make sure they understand that they are expected to help out in the house. Be specific:

Ask if they prefer to do yardwork, clean the kitchen, or dust and vacuum in the living room and dining room.

- With the help of your tenant, list the tasks that have to be done around the house. Then ask your tenant to take an equitable share of the tasks, indicating you will complete the remaining tasks. You may want to make a list of the tasks, under the name of the person assigned those duties, and post it on the refrigerator or household bulletin board.

- Divide the tasks by room such as kitchen, bathroom, living room/dining room. If you have, for example, two housemates, each of you might be responsible for cleaning one of the three areas each week, rotating the areas every week.

- If promised work is not being done, ask your tenants when they expect to get around to it. Set a time limit expectation.

- Hire someone else to do the housecleaning or the yardwork, and split the cost with your tenants.

SAMPLE CHART OF HOUSEHOLD TASKS

Barbara	Nancy	Doreen
Mow lawn.	Vacuum carpets.	Put trash outside.
Shovel snow.	Weed.	Clean garbage cans.
Clean sink/cabinets.	Rake.	Collect newspapers for pickup.
Clip hedges.	Clean porch	Clean refrigerator.
Clean toaster-oven.	Clean stove.	

Your Personal Food Supply Keeps "Disappearing."

- Make it absolutely clear which food supplies are to be shared by the household and which are for personal use only. For example, in some households, flour, sugar, salt, and spices are paid for collectively, and can be used by everyone. All other foods, though, may be only for the consumption of the person who bought them.

- Mark personal food supplies with the initials of the person to whom it belongs.
- Have separate shelves in the refrigerator and in kitchen cabinets for you and your tenants.
- Declare some food "fair game" for everyone in the household no matter who buys it. (In our household ice cream is "fair game" since I can't resist dipping into any ice cream in the house.)
- Have your own hiding place for the expensive liqueur or other delicacies which keep disappearing.
- Keep one eye half shut over the occasional disappearance of a slice of bread or a tablespoon of jam.

Your Tenant Is Bringing Home Boyfriends or Girlfriends to Spend the Night

- When you screen your potential tenants, make sure they understand the house rules regarding boyfriends and/or girlfriends spending the night. In my own household, I don't allow it, but will make an occasional exception for an out-of-town boyfriend. It's your house, and you are entitled to your own idiosyncrasies.
- Determine why the fact that a boyfriend or girlfriend staying overnight is bothering you—infringement on privacy? (It can be quite disconcerting to go to the bathroom at two in the morning and find a strange, naked man there.) Too much noise? (Have you ever tried to sleep when the plumbing keeps making repeated gurgling noises because of repeated showers and toilet flushing?) Having an additional car parked in the driveway? (What do you do when you have a morning meeting, your housemate and her boyfriend are still asleep or something, and his car is blocking yours in the driveway?) You may discover that your discomfort is not really caused by the fact that the boyfriend or girlfriend is sleeping overnight but by other factors associated with it. Your uneasiness may disappear if the guest

agrees not to park behind your car or if your housemate agrees to have her boyfriend sleep over no more than once a week. Explain the situation to your tenant and ask him or her to think of ways to minimize your discomfort.

- Suggest that your tenants visit their "friends" overnight at the friends' homes.

Your Tenant Is Not Paying Attention to Conserving Energy and Your Utility Bills Are Very High

- When a utility bill arrives, remark how high it is, and ask your tenant to think of any way the household can reduce energy consumption.
- Ask your tenant to remind you if you do anything which wastes energy, and suggest that you will do the same for him or her.
- Explain to your tenant which appliances use the most energy (e.g., dryers) and how much more it costs if the thermostat is set at 73 degrees rather than on 68 degrees in the winter if you live in a frost belt state.

Your Tenant Is Not Paying the Rent or the Utility Bills on Time

- When the utility bills arrive, mark the tenant's share on the bills and leave them in a conspicuous place such as the kitchen table. Don't remove them until the tenant has paid.
- After 2 or 3 days, remind a tenant that you must pay the mortgage and the utility bills, and you are just waiting for his or her check. Ask when you can expect it.
- Put a clause in your rental agreement stating that there will be a late charge of $10 if the tenant is more than 5 days late paying the rent or the utilities. Or, better, set the rent $10 higher than the amount you intended, and state in the rental agreement that if the tenant pays the rent on or before the first of the month, he or she will get a $10 rent reduction.

How to Terminate a Tenancy

If you have chosen a tenant with care, you should rarely, if ever, have to ask someone to leave. In fact, I have never had to ask a housemate to leave (knock wood).

But what do you do if the problems you are having with your tenant are insurmountable? Well, if it's just a personality clash, often both of you will feel the discomfort and the tenant may decide to move without any urging from you.

Let's say, though, that the problem is more dramatic. For example, you go out of town for a weekend, and when you come back, you find that your tenant had a wild party which left your home in shambles—cigarette burns on your wall-to-wall carpet, smashed furniture, gaping holes in the living room wall, and nothing left of your picture window but a few shards of jagged glass. Your tenant says that a few friends got out of hand.

Everyone's reaction would be different. When I am very angry, I get quiet—very quiet. I think I would say, "I'll have the insurance company send someone over so you'll know how much you'll have to pay for the damage." My next statement would be, "How fast can you get out of here?" No matter if your tenant says 5 days or a month, write a letter that day stating when the rental agreement is to be terminated and explain why, detailing the exact nature and extent of the damage. Immediately send the letter by certified mail. Be sure to keep a copy of the letter for yourself. When the need arises, you will have both a copy of the letter and the certified receipt as evidence.

Let's say that a month passes, and your tenant informs you that he or she couldn't find another place, and isn't going to leave. Although you may think that the simplest solution is to change the locks on the door when your tenant is out of the house, this tactic may not be legal, and your tenant may turn around and sue you. Your best bet is to phone your local government office and ask for the clerk of the court. Explain your situation, and find out the quickest legal procedure to remove the tenant from your house.

I hope this example doesn't scare you. I've never heard of a situation in which a tenant had to be forcibly removed from an owner's house. It's really a worst case scenario, and very unlikely to happen.

It is rare, but more probable, that you discover irreconcilable differences with your tenant over a period of a few months. If this occurs, "keep your cool," sit down, and have a chat. I'm assuming here that you have already discussed the problem with your tenant before, to no avail.

You may want to approach your tenant a day or so after the rent has been paid. You will then be in a position to give your tenant more than 30 days of notice without missing any rent, seeing you have that month's rent plus the amount that's been paid toward the last month's rent.

The chat may consist of five parts, and you would do well to rehearse it to yourself before speaking with your tenant:

- Open the conversation by saying something positive about the tenant.
- Relate the problem with the current situation without being accusatory.
- Explain that according to the terms of the rental agreement, you are allowed to give a tenant 30 days' notice to terminate the agreement.
- Let the tenant know when you will begin to advertise for a new tenant.
- Send the tenant written notice by certified mail.

The following is an example of a chat you might have:

"Arlene, could we sit down and talk? You have been with me now for four months. In a lot of ways I've appreciated having you as a tenant. You have pitched in with the household chores, and you have a terrific sense of humor which I've thoroughly enjoyed.

"However, for the past three months, the rent has come on the tenth or fifteenth of the month, and never on the first. Each time we talked about the late rent, you said that you had to make the payments on all your credit cards that month, but the rent would be paid on time in the future. This month you told me the same thing again. Although you finally paid the rent yesterday, on the seventeenth, I never know when you will pay the rent, and it is difficult for me to keep juggling my own finances to pay the mortgage.

"I like you, but I'm going to have to ask you to find another place to live. According to our rental agreement, I have to give you 30 days' notice. Is this enough time for you to find another place? [If not, allow the tenant some extra time to find other accommodations, provided you have enough of the last month's rent and security deposit to cover the additional period of time.]

"I will start advertising for a new tenant next weekend. Is there any time you would prefer that I not show your room? I'd like to inconvenience you as little as possible.

"One other thing—according to the terms of our rental agreement, I'm supposed to give you written notice. You should receive a certified letter in the mail in a day or two. I'm really sorry to have to do this."

It does not pay to antagonize a tenant. Generally, if you show yourself to be reasonable, your tenant will be reasonable in turn.

Happily, you may never have to terminate a rental agreement. Usually your tenants will let you know they will be moving because they are getting married, they are being transferred, or they've saved enough money to buy a condominium.

Make sure you have the tenant's new address so you can return the remainder of the security deposit after the last utility bills have come in and forward any mail that still comes to your address.

Your last official act as a landlord may be the return of the deposit with a cover letter itemizing the deductions along with copies of the bills.

You may, however, continue to exchange Christmas cards, invitations to housewarmings, birth announcements, and long-distance phone calls for years after they have left. Making money isn't the only reason for having tenants in your house.

December 8, 1986

Bill Parker
111 Main Street
Los Angeles, CA 90049

Hi Bill,

At last! The water and sewage bill came yesterday, which means all of the utility bills are in now. According to my calculations, your share came to $48.07, so I owe you $101.93 from your original deposit of $150.

Telephone	$13.91
Water & sewage	13.25
Gas	3.73
Electricity	17.18
TOTAL	$48.07

Please feel free to check my math against the enclosed bills. If you have any questions you can always get ahold of me.

Bill, I very much appreciated having you as a tenant these past two years. Good luck in California, and if you ever get to the east coast again, be sure to drop in.

Sincerely,

Doreen

Doreen Bierbrier

Enclosures

Points to Remember

1. Abide by a fair set of rules, both written and unwritten, and expect your tenant to do likewise.

2. Draw up a written rental agreement which is in conformance with the laws of your state and locality.

3. Remember that even though a signed rental agreement is legally binding, the agreement is only as good as the intentions of the people who sign it.

4. Make sure that your tenant understands the terms of the written and unwritten agreement from the outset, particularly in regard to:
   a. Security deposits
   b. Responsibility for repairs
   c. Insurance coverage
   d. Expected household behavior
   e. Rent increases

5. Try to resolve household problems by involving a tenant in suggesting a solution.

6. Get a departing tenant's forwarding address, and return the remainder of the security deposit, itemizing deductions, as soon as the last utility bills arrive.

4

THE TAX STRATEGY

The main reason for keeping many of the records pertaining to your rental is because you will need the information and documentation for tax purposes. Well-organized record keeping, however, will also keep your rental operation running more smoothly.

You can maintain all your records in two separate binders: one to keep track of essential household and rental documents and the other to keep track of financial transactions related to your renters.

What Household Information Should You Keep?

Your *Household Information Binder* should contain all essential information and documentation relating to your household and may include all or some of the following:

- Documents received at closing (settlement)
  - —Deed of sale
  - —Deed of trust
  - —Closing (settlement) sheet of expenses
  - —Purchase contract

61

—Plat survey

—House inspection report

—Appraisal

—Local covenants/condominium bylaws

—Insurance documents

- Correspondence related to the house/tenants
- Tenants' rental applications
- Rental agreements/agreements with contractors
- Property tax notices
- Insurance policies
- Warranties/guarantees
- Documentation of major improvements and/or casualty losses

Some of the information in this binder will be used from time to time during the year, when you want to refresh your memory about the terms of the rental agreement or to make sure what your insurance covers. You will need other material to document your closing charges, major home improvements, and casualty losses for tax purposes.

How to Keep Financial Records

You need to keep financial records both for your own knowledge and because the IRS requires owners who rent out part of their homes to report their rental income and expenditure.

Many people who share their houses with tenants neglect to mention their rental arrangement to the IRS. I do, and always have, partly because my father told me a long time ago, *"Don't mess with the IRS."*

Keeping records of financial transactions related to your rental is not that complicated. Determining a tax strategy is more complicated, as is trying to figure out what percentage of expenses and capital improvements are deductible, or if they are deductible at all. In fact, many seasoned tax advisers throw up their hands in frustration when asked to interpret the tax laws as they apply to shared residences.

It is not always clear how the IRS wants you to do your reporting. Further, tax laws change. I am not a tax lawyer, and I strongly urge you to consult a professional tax adviser rather than religiously follow my guidance. Nonetheless, let me take a shot at explaining my understanding of how to keep financial records.

Basically, you need to record all the income paid to you by your tenants and all your expenditures made in their behalf during the year. Be sure to put absolutely everything down.

Your records, then, should have two major sections: *income* and *expenses;* and, depending on your tax strategy, possibly a third section for *capital expenditure.*

I always sit down at the beginning of the year and construct a notebook with a few sheets of paper labeled "Income," "Expenses," and "Capital Expenditure" in which I'll record all financial transactions pertaining to my rental for the upcoming year. If you want to set up a do-it-yourself record-keeping system, buy a binder and use the forms in the back of this book as the format for each of your three categories; keep receipts of all your purchases in a manila envelope; and hang on to your cancelled checks to prove you paid the bills.

Income

A tenant's rent, utility payments, damage fees and late charges should be recorded as "Income."

The subsections under "Income," therefore, would be:

- Rent
- Utility Income
- Other Income (payment for damages, late fees, etc.)

Use a separate sheet of paper for each subsection, labeling one sheet of paper "Rent," another "Utility Income," and a third, "Other Income."

Your sheet for "Rent" might look like this:

Date	Name of Tenant	Explanation	Amount Paid	Amount of Deposit
1/1	Jill Smith	X Security deposit Last month's rent	$195.00 $195.00	$150.00
2/3	Jill Smith	X	$195.00	
3/2	Jill Smith	X	$195.00	
5/1	Nancy Jones	X Security deposit Last month's rent	$195.00 $195.00	$150.00
5/15	Jill Smith	Deposit returned		($150.00)
6/2	Nancy Jones	X	$195.00	
7/3	Nancy Jones	X	$195.00	

You can use a check mark or an X in the explanation column if the payment is just the regular rent. Otherwise, you may want to jot down why extra money was paid and returned.

The last column, "Deposit," would only be used twice for each tenant, once when the tenant moves in and once when you return the deposit after the tenant has left. Use brackets or parentheses around sums of money to indicate a subtraction from your account.

The reason for putting refundable deposits in a separate column is because they should not be included with the rest of your income when you report it to the IRS at the end of the year. Security deposits don't count as "income"; when you actually charge a tenant for some expense and take the money from the tenant's deposit, then that amount of money should be entered as income. If, however, you return a deposit in full to a tenant, the IRS neither wants to know about the collection nor the return of your security deposits.

Prepaid rent, however, is a different matter. If a tenant pays the last month's rent in advance, that amount is counted as income to you in the year you receive it.

Your next sheet, labeled "Utility Income," might look like this:

UTILITY INCOME			
Gas	Electricity	Water & Sewage	Telephone
Date *Amount*	*Date* *Amount*	*Date* *Amount*	*Date* *Amount*
1/3 $52.63	1/5 $17.23	1/15 $21.13	1/5 $7.50
2/4 53.21	2/8 16.52	4/18 18.25	2/3 7.50
3/2 46.72	3/7 17.01	7/12 19.13	3/3 7.50

As you can see, I don't bother to list the names of the tenants who paid their share of the utility bills. My tenants include payment of the utility bills with their rent checks. I make sure the amounts they owe for utilities that month are included in their rent checks, and just record their names in my "Rent" record.

You may want to add another column for tenants' names to my chart for "Utility Income" if your tenants pay their utility bills at different times during the month and you need help remembering whether a tenant has paid a share of the utility bills that month.

Let's go over some of the terms which appear in the chart.

"Date" refers to the date you receive payment from your tenant. "Amount" refers to the money you have collected from your tenant for the tenant's share of the utility bill and not to the amount you have paid the utility company. Income generated from utility payments by tenants will be offset later when you record part of the payments you make to the utility companies as a business expense.

The last sheet under "Income" is "Other Income." It might look like this:

OTHER INCOME			
Date	Tenant's Name	Reason for Payment	Amount
2/22	Jane Smith	Check bounced	$25
5/18	Jane Smith	Repair burn on kitchen floor	75
9/20	Jane Smith	Late rent charge	15

Expenses

You will have more kinds of expenses than you have sources of income. Income is usually limited to rent and utility payments. Under expenses, you may have the cost for ads, paint, carpet cleaning, plumbing repairs, and many other items.

You will need to record all the expenses associated with your rental in order to report them to the IRS. Rather than make up your own categories to organize your expenses, I suggest that you use the categories supplied to you by the IRS under Schedule E, *Supplemental Income Schedule*, "Rental and Royalty Expenses." You won't need to use all their categories as headings for your "Expenses" section, but you can select those categories for which you think you'll find the most use.

My records currently have the following subsections under "Expenses":

- Advertising
- Cleaning and Maintenance
- Repairs
- Supplies
- Utilities
- Other Expenses

In addition, I have other major expenses which I call "end-of-the-year expenses." These are for

- Homeowner's insurance
- Interest on my mortgage
- Property tax

I don't keep track of my expenditure for insurance, property tax, and interest on a monthly basis. Rather, I wait for my mortgage company to send me a statement at the end of the year for each of those three categories. As we shall see later, you will need to record part of your payments for insurance, interest, and taxes, on Schedule E and part of the interest and taxes on Schedule A, if you itemize your personal deductions.

Recording expenses is more complicated than recording income, because you have to determine what part of each expenditure was made in behalf of your tenants.

If you have a repair made on a fixture which is solely for your own use, you can't deduct any of the cost as a rental expense. On the other hand, if you pay for something which is solely in behalf of your tenants, you can deduct 100 percent as a rental expense. For example, you can deduct 100 percent of the cost of advertising to find a tenant, painting the tenant's room, or repairing plumbing used exclusively by your tenant.

Things start getting more complicated when both you and your tenant share some fixture, appliance, improvement, or furnishing. Some tax advisers say that only shared items which are considered to be your personal property can be partially deducted as a business expense, while shared "realty" cannot be considered a business expense. Let me explain.

"Realty" means something which is permanently affixed to the house, like a water heater, a furnace, or wall-to-wall carpeting. Personal property, or "personalty," usually means something that can be moved around, like furniture, a portable air-conditioning unit, or even a refrigerator, a washing machine, or a stove.

These advisers would say that if your tenant uses your personal property, you are entitled to write off part of the cost to repair or replace these items as a business expense. On the other hand, they would say that you can't write off any of the cost of repairing or maintaining realty which is not for the tenant's exclusive use. This hard-line position does not seem to be tenable, in that in at least one case (which we'll discuss later) the IRS did not question a deduction for the maintenance of a pool that the owner shared with his tenants or for yard maintenance.

It would seem, then, if you and your tenants both walk on a wall-to-wall living room carpet, the cost to clean the carpet could be partly deducted as a business expense. If you have one tenant, the split for the expense would be 50 percent deducted as a business expense. If you and your tenant use the kitchen sink equally, and after repeated use by both of you, the plumbing fixtures have to be replaced, again, 50 percent of the cost of the replacement could be recorded as a business expense. The same would be true of painting a room shared with your tenant.

In addition to allocating expenses between you and your tenant, you will at some point have to calculate how much of your house is being used for rental and how much is for your personal use, if only to apportion the interest on your house loan and property tax between Schedules A and E. You'll also need to figure out how much of your house is used for rental in order to determine what percent of your homeowner's insurance to record on Schedule E.

If you have two tenants, but they are only in a small portion of the house, you can't claim that two-thirds of your house is a rental and one-third is for your personal use. Rather, you have to find out exactly how much space your tenants are occupying.

To find out what percentage of your house is being rented, you can either measure the square footage of the rooms being used for rental purposes and compare it with the total square footage in the house; or you can count the number of rooms being rented in the house and compare it with the total number of rooms in the house to arrive at the percentage of the house which is considered owner-occupied.

There is some controversy about how to count (or if to count at all) those rooms you share with your tenants, such as living rooms, kitchens, dining rooms, recreation rooms, and bathrooms. At this point, the IRS position seems to be that you can only count rooms which are for the exclusive use of your tenants to determine what percentage of your house is being used to produce income. However, even this position is open to question as you will see when we discuss the *Semander* case later in this chapter.

Once you determine what percentage of the house is being used for rental you will be able to calculate what percentage of your interest, tax, and insurance will go on Schedule E and what percentage of interest and tax should be recorded on Schedule A—Schedule E for rental expenses, Schedule A for personal expenses.

Examples of Expenses

1. Advertising
   - Cost of placing an advertisement in the newspaper
   - Fees for posting rental notices
   - Fees for a roommate referral service

2. Cleaning and maintenance
   - Payment for cleaning of carpets
   - Payment for waxing of floors
   - Payment for window cleaning
   - Payment for cleaning of gutters and downspouts
   - Payment for maintenance of furnace, boiler, or air conditioner
   - Payment for painting of the interior or exterior of the house

3. Repairs
   - Payment for repair of a leak in the plumbing
   - Payment to patch a roof
   - Payment for fixing a loose banister
   - Payment for repair of washer, dryer, furnace, refrigerator

4. Supplies
   - Cost of carpet shampoo solution
   - Cost of wax for the floor
   - Cost of paint
   - Cost of books (like this one) which help you manage your rental

5. Utilities
   - Cost of gas
   - Cost of electricity
   - Cost of water and sewage
   - Cost of telephone service

6. Other expenses
   - Auto and travel (You may deduct the auto and travel expenses incurred because of your rental, such as when you pick up a potential tenant at the airport. Keep track of your mileage and multiply that figure, at the end of the year, by the amount the IRS permits you to use to estimate the cost per mile. In addition, you can claim the amount

you spent on parking and tolls if it was made in behalf of your rental.)

- Legal and professional fees (You may deduct expenses incurred, for example, when consulting a lawyer to draw up a rental agreement, or an accountant to set up a record-keeping system for your rental.)

Let's look at an example of one expense sheet, "Repairs":

REPAIRS				
Date	Service	% as Rental Expense	Cost	Amount Claimed
2/18	Open blocked drain in tenant's sink	100%	$50	$50
4/12	Repair washer	50%	$150	$75
8/3	Patch roof	25%	$60	$15

In the above example, the owner is sharing a house with one tenant who shares the washing machine with the owner. According to the owner's calculations, the tenant occupies one-fourth of the house.

Capital Expenditure and Depreciation

"Capital expenditure" and "depreciation" are more complicated concepts to grasp than "expenses" or "income." As I'll explain later, depending on your circumstances and your tax strategy, you may not need to calculate your depreciation at all.

If you plan to let your tax adviser complete your tax forms, you just need to read the next few pages in order to find out what "capital expenditure" and "depreciation" mean. Then keep track of your capital expenditure on a chart like this:

CAPITAL EXPENDITURE		
Date Purchased	Item	Total Cost
2/4/81	House (*less* land)	$82,468*
5/18/81	Refrigerator	687
9/30/81	Sofa	726
4/23/83	Furnace	1,982

*Your tax preparer can calculate the total cost of your house for tax purposes.

Your tax preparer will be able to help you from there, determining how much depreciation you will be able to take each year, if any, for each item.

What Is Depreciation and What Is a Capital Expenditure?

Basically, the IRS assumes that major items called "capital improvements" will wear out over time and have to be replaced. If these items are used in the production of income, each year the IRS will allow you to deduct the amount of the loss, or "depreciation," you have incurred for the item that is wearing out.

Using the IRS definition, you may claim depreciation on that part of your house used to produce rental income. Please note, however, that while your house is partially depreciable, the land on which it is built does not wear out and, thus, is not depreciable.

In addition to the house itself, you may claim depreciation on furniture, carpeting, major appliances, major fixtures, and other major improvements made to the house depending if the improvement is for the sole use of your tenant or, depending on your tax strategy, to the extent to which your tenants benefit from the capital expenditure.

Here are some examples of capital improvements:

- The house itself (minus the land)
- Furnace

- Washer
- Dryer
- Water heater
- Refrigerator
- Installation of a patio
- Conversion of an unfinished basement into an accessory dwelling unit
- Replacement of a roof
- Installation of a new kitchen floor

In order for you to determine how much depreciation you can take for your capital improvements, you first have to determine how much the improvement is worth, or its "basis." The IRS provides clear guidelines on how to determine basis.

What Is the "Basis" of Your Property?

Your house probably will be the single most expensive capital improvement you have to depreciate. If you have just bought a house and rent it out immediately, the "basis" of your house is the purchase price, *plus* acquisition costs which include the cost for insuring and clearing the title, points paid (depending if they were prepaid interest or not), fees for negotiating the purchase, legal and accounting fees for acquisition of the property and protection of the title, cost of the survey, and appraisal fees.

If you have owned the house for awhile, you have to adjust the cost basis of your house, adding to your purchase price closing costs which were not tax deductible at the time of purchase and the cost of any capital improvements made since you bought the house, and subtracting any depreciation you may have taken in previous years and any casualty losses. When you start to rent to tenants after you have owned your house for a few years, the IRS says you can use as the basis either the adjusted cost basis of the house or the fair market value of the house at the time you took in renters—*whichever is less*.

After determining the cost basis of your house, or the adjusted cost basis, you must subtract the value of your nondepreciable land.

If you own a condominium, your home-to-land ratio may be 95 to 5. Depending on the area and the kind of residence you buy, the house-to-land ratio may vary considerably, with land value being anywhere from 5 to 65 percent of the total value of the property. Usually, the IRS will go along with your estimate, provided it seems reasonable. However, it is possible for the IRS to ask you to explain the objective criteria you used to make your house-to-land ratio.

There are several ways to figure out the ratio. One way to calculate the house-to-land ratio is to look at the property tax assessment of your house the year you take in your first renter. See what percentage of the assessment went toward the land and what percentage went toward the house.

For example, you buy a house and take in a renter that first year. Your purchase price, including acquisition costs, was $100,000. The assessed value of the house is $110,000, of which $50,000 is allocated to the land and $60,000 to the house. The land is therefore about 45.4 percent of the value of the entire property ($50,000 divided by $110,000). The basis of the house itself, then, without the land would be $54,600 (54.6 percent of your purchase price of $100,000).

How to Calculate Depreciation for Your House

Once you have calculated the basis of your house, minus the land, and you have figured out what percentage of the house is being used for rental purposes either by counting rooms or by the square-footage method, you can start to figure out how much depreciation you can take on your house.

You only need one more piece of information which you can get from IRS guidelines. You have to find out over how many years the IRS will let you depreciate the house.

If you shared your house with renters before 1981, the IRS permitted you to take depreciation in several ways including what is called the "straight-line method."

With the straight-line method of depreciation, an owner figures out the basis of the house, divides it by the useful life of the property (which is often estimated at 20 or 30 years), and then deducts the same amount for depreciation every year. For example, if an entire house was rented out and the basis of the house was $60,000, an owner could deduct $3000 per year if the house had a useful life of 20 years.

If you bought a house and started to share your house with renters between January 1, 1981, and March 15, 1984, you were allowed to take depreciation on the rented portion of your house over a 15-year period using the Accelerated Cost Recovery System (ACRS). The Tax Reform Act of 1984 raised the 15-year period to 18 years if you placed rental real property in service after March 15, 1984, and before May 9, 1985. After May 8, 1985, income-producing real property was put on a 19-year depreciation schedule as a result of the Imputed Interest Act of 1985.

As you can see, the tax laws keep changing. The only advice I can give you is to check the explanations in IRS Publication 527, "Rental Property," and look at the schedules given to you to find out the number of years you should take when you depreciate your house.

Just to give you an example, though, let's say you bought a house and got a renter for your basement apartment in March 1983. You have determined that the cost basis of your house (minus the land) is $50,875; your entire house has 10 rooms of which 4 are used exclusively by your renter. In other words 40 percent of the house is being used for rental purposes. You look at the IRS Schedule contained in IRS Publication 527, "Rental Property," and determine that the IRS permits you to take 11 percent of the basis of the house (just the rental part) for depreciation that first year.

These are the calculations you would make:

Basis of the house (rental portion) = $50,875 × 40%, or $20,350

Amount of depreciation to be claimed in 1983 would equal 11 percent of $20,350, or $2,239.

If you owned your house and had renters with you before 1981, you have to continue to depreciate the property using your older depreciation method. You also cannot use the newer methods of depreciation if you owned property that you held strictly for personal use before 1981. You'll have to use an older method, like straight-line depreciation. However, you *must* use the newer methods of calculating depreciation if you bought a house and got tenants to share your house after 1980.

How to Calculate the Basis of Other Capital Improvements

It is much easier to calculate the basis of other capital improvements such as a water heater, washing machine, or dining room table. The basis of these items is simply the purchase price. Again, you have to multiply the basis by the percentage of use by your tenants. If, for example, you have one tenant who shares the washer equally with you, and you paid $500 for a new washer, one-half of the cost, or $250, is an expenditure associated with your rental.

Checking IRS guidelines, you will determine what the estimated life of these major appliances, furnishings, or improvements would be. Let's say it is 5 years for a washer. Looking at IRS charts, you could deduct 15 percent of that $250, or $38, that first year as a business expense.

If you want to figure out depreciation yourself, you may want to keep records which look like this:

CAPITAL EXPENDITURE					
Date Purchased	Item	Total Cost or Basis	% for Rental	Life	Amount Claimed
3/15/83	House (less land)	$50,875	40%, or $20,350	15 yr @ 10%	$2,035
3/18/83	Washer	$500	50%, or $250	5 yr @ 15%	$38

Tax Strategies

Now that we've discussed the mechanics of record keeping, let's turn to formulating an overall tax strategy.

Ideally, you would like to allocate as much as possible of the cost of running your house to your rental, so you can deduct the expenses, and reduce your taxable income.

There are two major tax-related questions many people ask when trying to find every legitimate deduction they can take in connection with their rental. And the answers are not completely clear to many owners of shared houses. These are:

1. "Can you include, as part of your rental area, rooms that you share with your tenants?"
2. "Can you show a loss after you have calculated your rental income and offset it with your expenses and depreciation?"

Tax Strategies for Accessory Dwelling Units or Boarding Houses

Your tax strategy is easier to determine if you live in a duplex or have a separate accessory dwelling unit which is exclusively for the use of your tenant. You don't have to worry about shared living areas. You can treat the entire rental unit as a business proposition and, with no challenge from the IRS, fill out Schedule E claiming deductions in excess of your rental income.

Similarly, the tax codes allow a rental loss if you have a room or rooms in your house which you regularly rent out to boarders such as tourists or college students. Again, though, the rooms must be for the exclusive use of your boarders.

Tax Strategies for Shared Houses

What happens, though, if you rent out a room to a tenant who also shares a common living area with you, and your house is the tenant's principal place of residence? Your situation then becomes more complicated.

According to some IRS rulings, your property would then fall under Section 280A of the Tax Code, entitled "Disallowances of Certain Expenses in Connection with the Business Use of Home, Rental of Vacation Homes, etc." In shortened form, Section 280A is also known as "The Vacation Home Law."

At first glance, it appears that all owners who rent to tenants who live with the owner, sharing common living areas, would fall under Section 280A and be bound by its rules. The Vacation Home Law states that a taxpayer who rents out a dwelling unit but uses the dwelling unit for more than 14 days or for more than 10 percent of the number of days during the year for which the unit is rented at fair market value falls under that law. Further, Section 280A goes on to say that the rental of your house is subject to the "exclusive use" test. In other words, when calculating how much space is allocated for rental purposes, you cannot allocate any amount toward rooms which you share with your tenants.

Section 280A also states that if your property falls within its provisions, your expenses are deductible only up to the amount of the rental income you receive. And, in addition, you must deduct your rental expenses in the following order and stop once your income is offset by your expenses, reporting on Schedule E:

1. Interest, taxes, and casualty losses that are for the rental use (The part for your personal use would be recorded on Schedule A.)

2. Operating expenses in connection with your rental, except depreciation and other basis adjustments

3. Depreciation and other basis adjustments connected with the rental portion of your home

As you can see, the tax benefits of the Vacation Home Law are not particularly exciting. Although you can offset your rental income with expenses, you can't declare a loss and shelter income from other sources. In addition, that part of the interest and property tax you write off as a business expense could just as easily have been written off on Schedule A as a deductible expense anyway, even if the property was purely for your own personal use. So you won't get an additional tax savings when you divide your interest payments and tax payments between Schedules A and E.

As a side note, though, you can deduct part of the interest and property tax for business purposes on Schedule E and still take the full standard deduction if you decide not to itemize on Schedule A.

The Case of Zane John Semander

The IRS position that Section 280A covers situations in which a taxpayer shares a residence with a renter has been challenged by several sources: one, in a court case.

Zane John Semander filed a tax return in 1977 in which he declared that he had received rental income of $1650 from a tenant who shared his three-bedroom house in Houston, Texas, with him. Semander, however, claimed expenses and depreciation in the amount of $2122, taking a total tax loss.

Both Semander and his tenant had access to and use of the whole house and the pool during 1977. Semander attributed 35 percent of the total household expenses to the rental, including expenses for maintaining spaces which he shared with his tenant such as the swimming pool and the yard. In addition, he calculated depreciation by including a percentage of those rooms which he shared with his tenant.

The lawyer representing the IRS agreed that the 35 percent total for the house was correctly attributable to the tenant. The sole issue was whether the taxpayer was entitled to declare rental expenses in excess of his rental income.

The court ruled in favor of the IRS, deciding that Section 280A did apply and that deductible rental expenses were limited to the amount of rental income less deductions (such as interest and taxes) that would be allowed regardless of business use.

It should be noted, however, that Semander's defense may not have been as strong as it could have been, as he did not have the assistance of either an attorney or a tax accountant to help him with his case. Further, the decision was a Tax Court Memorandum, which technically is not considered to be precedent-setting.

That said, the *Semander* decision is on record and stands until another court case comes along.

More Aggressive Tax Strategies

You are unlikely to be questioned by the IRS if you follow the rules under Section 280A if you share your house with renters. There are, however, more aggressive strategies you can employ, although you should realize that the IRS may not agree with you if your return is audited, in which case a court may have to decide who is right, you or the IRS.

There is still a question if it was really congressional intent to have shared houses fall under the Vacation Home Law. Steven Rice suggested in a stimulating article for *The Journal of Real Estate Taxation*, in 1981, "that the Internal Revenue Service may be taking a position in this area which is unsupported by law." Analyzing the wording of the law, Rice shows that 280A was meant to apply to situations in which owners made personal use of a property before or after a rental, but not simultaneously with renters. Congress did not appear to consider a situation in which owners shared a house with renters at the same time. He suggests that Congress, in passing the law, was really trying to prevent taxpayers from taking a significant tax shelter from property which was not really being used primarily for business purposes, as much as it was for personal pleasure.

He also shows that "subsection (d) [of the law] provides an exception to the '14-day/10 percent test' by making the test inapplicable to a taxpayer who rents out a unit for a qualified rental period." Therefore, he concludes, that if owners rent out property for the entire year, they have a "qualified rental period" and would not fall under Section 280A in any event. The Vacation Home Law, he would say, simply was not designed to address housesharing.

If Rice is correct, a taxpayer with housemates would not be governed by the Vacation Home Law and would be free to use other tax strategies. He suggests that owners could record their financial transactions as a business on Schedule C, instead of Schedule E, and use the hobby loss rules. In other words, taxpayers could show a loss from their rental for 3 out of 5 years.

I would like to suggest another strategy, which to me seems more logical in certain instances. Let's say that a taxpayer buys a house with the intention of renting out rooms, although he or she intends to live in the house too. The house, then, was bought partly as an income-producing investment, rather than just a personal residence. Or, let's say, at some point in a person's life, the owner decides to rent out some rooms, thereby converting part of a principal residence to an investment property.

It seems to me, then, that the owner should be able to report all financial transactions to the IRS just as he or she would for any other investment property. The owner would use Schedule E to report all income, expenses, and depreciation, for that portion of the house used for rental purposes. The owner could take a loss and continue to declare a loss, year after year, just as with any other investment house.

Assuming that 280A does not apply to shared residences, the owner would allocate all the space used strictly by renters, and might allocate a percentage of rooms that were shared with the owner to business purposes, arguing that the "exclusive use test" was not applicable. If the owner and one tenant, for example, shared the living room, dining room, and kitchen equally, the split on those rooms would be allocated at 50 percent for personal use and 50 percent for business use.

As you can see from the above discussion, choosing a tax strategy is no easy matter and one that you will want to discuss with your tax adviser.

What Are the Tax Consequences When You Sell Your House after Having Shared It with Renters?

Our tax laws have given people various incentives for buying their own homes. You can, for example, deduct your interest payments for home mortgages as well as property taxes on Schedule A. Another major incentive is that the federal government will defer taxing the profit you make when you sell a personal residence if you buy another house of greater or equal value within a certain period of time. Then, at the age of 55 or older, an owner can sell a personal residence and shelter up to a certain amount of profit ($125,000 as of this writing) that has accumulated in several homes over the years.

What happens, though, if you are using part of your personal residence to produce rental income? If you have a renter in your house in the year of the sale, you will have to report the sale to the IRS as if it were two separate sales.

To do this, determine how much of your residence is for your own personal use and how much is used by your renter. Only the percentage you use will qualify for the tax benefits accorded to the owner of a personal residence. The sale of the "business" part of your house will not fall under the rollover "residence replacement rule" but instead under the tax rules governing capital gains.

However, let's say that after having rented out part of your house for several years, you decide not to have renters any longer. You convert the entire house back to your own personal residence and use the rooms previously occupied by your renters for your own use.

If the sale of your house occurs in that year when you no longer had any part of your house being used for business or rental purposes and it was being used strictly as your personal residence, you do not have to handle the sale of your house as though it were two separate transactions. You would have to factor in any depreciation you may have taken over the years while you had renters in your house, but 100 percent of the purchase price would fall under the favorable rules which govern the sale of personal residences.

Please note, however, if you are 55 or older and plan to use the once-in-a-lifetime exclusion, you must convert your entire house back to your personal residence *for 3 out of the last 5 years before the sale* if your whole house is to qualify for that preferential tax treatment.

One Final Note about the Tax Implications

Do not let the tax laws scare you. Get assistance from a professional tax adviser who will assist you in taking every tax advantage to which you are legally entitled.

Points to Remember

1. Maintain two binders—one for essential household and rental documents and the other to keep track of financial transactions.
2. Keep the following in your House Information Binder:
   a. Documents received at closing (settlement)
   b. Correspondence related to the house/tenants
   c. Rental agreements/agreements with contractors
   d. Property tax notices
   e. Insurance policies
   f. Warranties/guarantees
   g. Documentation of major improvements/additions made to the house
3. Keep financial records for tax purposes which contain the following information:
   a. Income
      (1) Rent
      (2) Utility income
      (3) Other

    b. Expenses
        (1) Advertising
        (2) Cleaning and maintenance
        (3) Repairs
        (4) Supplies
        (5) Utilities
        (6) Other
    c. Capital expenditure
        (1) Realty
        (2) Personalty

4. Consult your tax adviser to make sure you have taken every deduction to which you are legally entitled.

5

WHERE DO WE GO FROM HERE?

Well, dear reader, I hope this book has provided you with some practical step-by-step guidance on how to share your home with tenants.

You will find that living with tenants will be rewarding (financially and otherwise), frustrating, mellowing, interesting, and educational—and you can experience this right in your own home. What better nonbusiness to have!

If you've just been thinking about sharing your house with tenants—what are you waiting for? As my father always says, *"You won't catch any fish if you don't put your hook in the water."*

Go to it, and good luck!

BIBLIOGRAPHY

For those of you who would like to read other publications on this subject, I highly recommend the following:

1. *Managing Your Rental House for Increased Income*, by Doreen Bierbrier (McGraw-Hill, 1985), a lively and comprehensive guide (if I do say so myself) on how to buy and manage single-family houses for greatly increased rental income by renting to singles.

2. *The Rights of Tenants*, by Richard E. Blumberg and James R. Grow (Avon, 1978), an excellent national survey of the legal rules of the rental game, although definitely written from the tenant's viewpoint.

3. *The Group House Handbook*, by Nancy Brandwein, Jill MacNeice, and Peter Spiers (Acropolis, 1982), a book about house sharing, oriented toward renters sharing a house with other renters, which is full of personal anecdotes and some practical tips.

4. *Real Estate Principles*, Second Edition by Bruce Harwood (Reston Publishing Company, 1980), a readable summary of important real estate concepts, some of which would be of particular importance to landlords, e.g., essentials of a valid contract, insurance, rental marketing strategies, etc.

5. *How to Manage Real Estate Successfully—In Your Spare Time*, by Albert J. Lowry (Simon & Schuster, 1977), a complete book on the management of apartment buildings. People sharing their homes with tenants can apply some of the information to their own situations.

6. *Landlording*, by Leigh Robinson (Express, 1980), a humorous and practical guide to selecting tenants, managing small apartment buildings, and making repairs.

84

BIBLIOGRAPHY

You may also want to order the following free publications from the IRS:

Publication 17, "Your Federal Income Tax"

Publication 527, "Rental Property"

Publication 530, "Tax Information for Homeowners"

Publication 551, "Basis of Assets"

Publication 587, "Business Use of Your Home"

The most important of these, for your purposes is Publication 527 "Rental Property." You can obtain IRS publications by phoning your local IRS office and requesting them.

In addition to these practical publications, I found *The Third Wave* by Alvin Toffler (Bantam, 1980) presents a fascinating explanation why in the future many American households will no longer consist of a husband, a wife, and children. Rather, we'll be seeing more households shared by people with diverse relationships to each other.

APPENDIX A

AN OWNER'S PACKET OF RENTAL FORMS

House Information Sheet
Utilities Expense Worksheet
List of Callers
Tenant Application Form
Rental Agreement
Financial Record-Keeping Forms

HOUSE INFORMATION SHEET

ROOM	DIMENSIONS
Living Room	
Dining Room	
Kitchen	
Bedroom (Rental)	
Other Rooms:	

Average Utility Bills per Month

Gas   _____

Electric   _____

Water &

     Sewage _____

TOTAL   _____

Tenant's share @ _____% = _____ per month

Distance to Public Transportation? _____

           to Shopping? _____

           to Groceries _____

           to Downtown _____

Frequency of Bus/Subway Service? _____

UTILITIES EXPENSE WORKSHEET

Year _____	Oil	Gas	Electricity	Water & Sewage
January				
February				
March				
April				
May				
June				
July				
August				
September				
October				
November				
December				

Yearly
Totals ☐ ☐ ☐ ☐

Divide each total by 12.

Average/Mo ☐ ☐ ☐ ☐

LIST OF CALLERS

Date	Name	Home Tel.	Office Tel.	Comments	Appt.

TENANT APPLICATION FORM

1. Name of Prospective Tenant _____
2. Home No. _____ Office No. _____
3. Present Occupation _____
4. Name and Address of Firm _____
   _____
   _____

5. Name of Supervisor _____
   Telephone Number of Supervisor _____
6. Previous Occupation (if employed less than 6 months at present job) _____
7. Name of Previous Supervisor _____
   Telephone No. of Previous Supervisor _____
8. Address(es) of Applicant for Last 2 Years

Address	Dates	Landlord	Telephone No.

9. Name, Address, and Phone Number of Nearest Relative

_____ _____ _____
        Name   Address   Phone

10. Name and Phone Number of Two Friends Locally

_____ _____
              Name   Phone

_____ _____
              Name   Phone

COMMENTS:

RENTAL AGREEMENT

This agreement has been entered into on _____ _____, by and between _____, hereinafter called Tenant and _____ _____, hereinafter called Owner.

In consideration of a monthly rent of $____ plus ____% of the utilities (specifically for gas, electricity, water, trash collection, and basic telephone service) the Tenant will be entitled to share, on a month-to-month basis, the residence located at _____.

The following are mutually agreed upon points:

1. Tenant will begin tenancy on _____.
2. Rent will be due on the _____ day of every month.
3. Tenant will pay the first month's rent and an equal sum toward the last month's rent before moving in.
4. Tenant will pay a security deposit of $_____ before moving in. Within ____ days after departure if all obligations have been paid in full, and if the premises have been maintained in satisfactory condition, the Tenant's deposit, together with any interest required by law, will be returned to the Tenant. Any deductions will be itemized in writing and sent to the Tenant.
5. The initial utility bill and the last month's utility bill will be prorated to coincide with the number of days that the Tenant has agreed to occupy the house (i.e., until the last day of the rental period for that month). Otherwise, no matter how many days the Tenant is away from the house during the course of a month, the Tenant is responsible for ____% of the utility bills.
6. Tenant is not permitted to sublet the premises without the express consent of the Owner.
7. Tenant shall make no alterations, additions, or improvements to the premises without the express consent of the Owner.

8. Owner is responsible for paying for the major maintenance, cleaning, and repair of the furnace, roof, water heater, central air conditioning, gutters and outside plumbing, and repairs to major equipment and appliances when used in the course of their normal and proper usage.
9. Tenant is responsible for keeping plumbing fixtures as clean and safe as condition permits, shall unstop and keep clear all waste pipes which are for the Tenant's exclusive use, and will pay for any loss or damage caused by his or her negligence.
10. Owner shall not be liable to Tenant, unless required by law, for any damage or injury to the Tenant nor to the Tenant's guests, nor for any personal property which is stolen or damaged due to flooding, leaks, malfunction of equipment, structural problems, or for any reason whatever. All persons and personal property on said premises associated with the Tenant will be the sole risk and responsibility of the Tenant.
11. This agreement and the tenancy hereby granted may be terminated at any time by either party hereto by giving to the other party not less than 30 days' prior notice in writing. Terminations initiated by the Tenant must end on the last day of the month.

Special Provisions:

Both parties have read this agreement, agree to its terms, and each has a copy.

| _____ | _____ |
| TENANT | OWNER |

FINANCIAL RECORD-KEEPING FORMS
RENTAL RECORD
198_

Income
Expenses
Capital Expenditure

INCOME

Rent
Utility Income
Other Income

RENT (198_)

Date	Name of Tenant	Explanation	Amount Paid	Amount of Deposit

Total Rent for 198 __

UTILITY INCOME (198__)

Gas		Oil		Electricity		Water & Sewage		Telephone Basic Service	
Date	Amount	Date	Amount	Date	Amount	Date	Amount	Date	Amount

Yearly Totals
Gas _____
Oil _____
Electricity _____
Water & Sewage _____
Telephone _____

97

OTHER INCOME (198_)

Date	Tenant's Name	Reason for Payment	Amount

Total "Other Income" _____

EXPENSES

Advertising
Cleaning and Maintenance
Repairs
Supplies
Utilities
Other Expenses
Capital Expenditure

ADVERTISING (198_)

Date	Item	% as Rental Expense	Cost	Amount Claimed
			Total:	

CLEANING & MAINTENANCE (198_)

Date	Service	% as Rental Expense	Cost	Amount Claimed
			Total:	

REPAIRS (198_)

Date	Service	% as Rental Expense	Cost	Amount Claimed
		Total:		

SUPPLIES (198_)

Date	Item	% as Rental Expense	Cost	Amount Claimed
		Total:		

UTILITY EXPENSES (198__)

Gas		Oil		Electricity		Water & Sewage		Telephone Basic Service	
Date	Amount	Date	Amount	Date	Amount	Date	Amount	Date	Amount

Yearly Totals

Gas _____

Oil _____

Electricity _____

Water & Sewage _____

Telephone _____

Basic Service _____

Grand Total _____

% as Rental Expense _____

Amount Claimed _____

OTHER EXPENSES (198_)

1. Auto and Travel (mileage × cost per mile) _____
2. Commissions _____
3. Insurance × % attributed to rental _____
4. Interest × % attributed to rental _____
5. Legal and Other Professional Fees _____
6. Taxes × % attributed to rental _____
7. Wages and Salary × % attributed to rental _____
8. Other _____

CAPITAL EXPENDITURE (198_)

Date Pur-chased	Item	Total Cost or Basis	% for Rental	Amount Claimed	Tax Life

APPENDIX B

SUMMARY CHART OF STATE FAIR HOUSING LAWS*

States

Types of Discrimination Prohibited	AK	CA	CO	CT	DE	DC	FL	HI	ID	IL	IN	IA	KN	KY	ME	MD
Race	x	x	x	x	x	x	x	x	x	x	x	x	x	x	x	x
Color	x	x	x	x	x	x	x	x	x	x	x	x	x	x	x	x
National Origin	x	x	x	x	x	x	x		x	x	x	x	x	x	x	x
Sex	x	x	x	x	x	x	x	x	x	x	x	x	x	x	x	x
Religion	x	x	x			x	x	x	x	x	x	x	x	x	x	x
Ancestry		x	x	x			x			x	x		x		x	
Creed			x	x	x							x				
Physical Disability				x			x			x			x		x	x
Mental Disability										x					x	x
Disability/Handicap		x			x	x					x	x				
Marital Status	x	x	x	x	x	x		x		x						x
Age	x			x	x	x				x						x
Mental Retardation				x												
Familial Responsibility						x										
Parental/Family Status															x	
Veteran Status/Member of Armed Forces																
Blindness				x												
Nationality																
Deafness				x												

* Compiled from *Directory of State and Local Fair Housing Agencies,* U.S. Commission on Civil Righ
Clearinghouse Publication 86, March 1985 which contains summaries of laws from 37 states t
have fair housing laws and agencies which enforce them. The chart reflects the written law, and
necessarily the law of each state as interpreted by the courts.

104

MT	MN	MO	MT	NE	NV	NH	NJ	NM	NY	NC	OH	OR	PA	RI	SD	TN	VA	WA	WV	WI
X	X	X	X	X	X	X	X	X	X	X	X	X	X	X	X	X	X	X	X	X
X	X	X	X	X	X	X	X	X	X	X	X	X	X	X	X	X	X	X	X	X
X	X	X	X	X	X	X	X	X	X	X	X	X	X	X	X	X	X	X	X	X
X	X	X	X	X	X	X	X	X	X	X	X	X	X	X	X	X	X	X	X	X
X	X	X	X	X	X	X		X		X	X	X	X	X	X	X		X	X	X
	X				X		X	X			X		X	X	X				X	X
X	X	X	X	X	X	X	X	X	X	X	X	X	X	X	X	X	X	X	X	X
	X	X	X			X	X	X	X			X	X	X				X	X	X
	X	X	X			X	X	X	X			X						X	X	X
											X		X							
X	X					X	X	X			X			X				X		X
X		X				X		X						X						X
	X																			
							X												X	
							X													
							X													

SUMMARY CHART OF STATE FAIR HOUSING LAWS
(*Continued*)

States

	AK	CA	CO	CT	DE	DC	FL	HI	ID	IL	IN	IA	KN	KY	ME	MD
Use of Guide Dog				x												
Presence of Children				x												
Parenthood	x															
Changes in Marital Status	x															
Pregnancy	x															
Unfavorable Discharge from Military										x						
Personal Appearance						x										
Sexual Orientation						x										
Political Affiliation						x										
Place of Residence/Business						x										
Matriculation						x										
Source of Income						x										
Public Assistance																

Types of Discrimination Prohibited

106

Appendix B

MT	MN	MO	MT	NE	NV	NH	NJ	NM	NY	NC	OH	OR	PA	RI	SD	TN	VA	WA	WV	WI
							x						x					x		
																				x
																				x
	x																			

APPENDIX C

STATES WHICH EXEMPT OWNER-OCCUPIED DWELLINGS FROM STATE FAIR HOUSING LAWS*

State	Exemption for Owner-Occupant	Exemption
AK	No	None found. State Commission for Human Rights.
CA	Yes	"The term 'discrimination' does not include refusal to rent or lease a portion of an owner-occupied single-family house to a person as a roomer or boarder living within the household, provided that no more than one roomer or boarder is to live within the household."
CO	Yes	". . . 'housing' does not include any room offered for rent or lease in a single-family dwelling maintained and occupied in part by the owner or lessee of said dwelling as his household."
CT	Yes	"The provisions of this section shall not apply (A) to the rental of a housing accommodation in a building which contains housing accommodations for not more than two families living independently of each other, if the

* This chart reflects the letter of the law as reported in Prentice-Hall, *Equal Opportunity in Housing Series,* Section on State Laws, and does not necessarily reflect the law of each state as interpreted by the courts.

STATES WHICH EXEMPT OWNER-OCCUPIED DWELLINGS FROM STATE FAIR HOUSING LAWS
(*Continued*)

State	Exemption for Owner-Occupant	Exemption
		owner or members of his family reside in one of such housing accommodations, or (B) to the rental of a room or rooms in a housing accommodation, if such rental is by the occupant of the housing accommodation, or by the owner of the housing accommodation and he or a member of his family resides in such housing accommodation."
DE	Yes	"[An exception is made for] . . . rooms or units in dwellings containing living quarters occupied or intended to be occupied by no more than four families living independently of each other, if the owner thereof actually maintains and occupies one of such living quarters as his residence."
DC	Yes	"Nothing in this act is to be construed to apply to the rental or leasing of housing accommodations in a building in which the owner, or members of his family, occupy one of the living units and in which there are, or the owner intends that there be, accommodations for not more than: (1) Five (5) families, and only with respect to a prospective tenant, not related to the owner-occupant, with whom the owner-occupant anticipates the necessity of sharing a kitchen or a bath; and (2) Two (2)

STATES WHICH EXEMPT OWNER-OCCUPIED
DWELLINGS FROM STATE FAIR HOUSING LAWS
(Continued)

State	Exemption for Owner-Occupant	Exemption
		families living independently of each other."
FL	Yes	"Nothing . . . shall apply to: (b) rooms or units in dwellings containing living quarters occupied or intended to be occupied by no more than four families living independently of each other, if the owner actually maintains and occupies one of such living quarters as his residence."
GA	Yes	"Further, the provisions of this Act shall not apply to the rental or lease of any housing units in a housing accommodation which is occupied as a residence by the owner or a member of the owner's family."
HI	Yes	"[The law] . . . does not apply: (1) To the rental of a housing accommodation in a building which contains housing accommodations for not more than two families living independently of each other if the lessor or a member of his family resides in one of the housing accommodations; or (2) to the rental of a room or rooms in a housing accommodation by an individual if he or a member of his family resides therein."
ID	Yes	"The provisions . . . do not apply (a) to the rental of a housing accommodation in a building which contains housing accommodations for not

STATES WHICH EXEMPT OWNER-OCCUPIED
DWELLINGS FROM STATE FAIR HOUSING LAWS
(Continued)

State	Exemption for Owner-Occupant	Exemption
		more than two (2) families living independently of each other, if the lessor or a member of his family resides in one (1) of the housing accommodations, or (b) to the rental of a room or rooms in a housing accommodation by an individual if he or a member of his family resides therein."
IL	Yes	"Exceptions. (B) Rental of a housing accommodation in a building which contains housing accommodations for not more than five families living independently of each other, if the lessor or a member of his or her family resides in one of the housing accommodations; (C) Private Rooms. Rental of a room or rooms in a private home by an owner if he or she or a member of his or her family resides therein or, while absent for a period of not more than 12 months."
IN	?	It appears as if a single-family house would not be categorized as a "public accommodation." "All persons within the jurisdiction of this state shall be entitled to the full and equal accommodations in every place of public accommodation . . . ; and any denial of such accommodation by reason of race, creed, or color of the applicant therefore shall be a violation of the provision of this section. A

111

STATES WHICH EXEMPT OWNER-OCCUPIED
DWELLINGS FROM STATE FAIR HOUSING LAWS
(*Continued*)

State	Exemption for Owner-Occupant	Exemption
		place of public accommodation . . . means any establishment, which caters or offers its services or facilities or goods to the general public including but not limited to, public housing projects."
IA	Yes	"The provisions . . . shall not apply to: (2) The rental or leasing of a housing accommodation in a building which contains housing accommodations for not more than two families living independently of each other, if the owner or members of his family reside in one of such housing accommodations. (3) The rental or leasing of less than six rooms within a single housing accommodation by the occupant or owner of such housing accommodation, if he or members of his family reside therein."
KS	Yes	"Nor shall anything in this act apply to rooms or units in buildings containing living quarters occupied or intended to be occupied by no more than four (4) families living independently of each other, if the owner actually maintains and occupies one of such living quarters as his residence."
KY	Yes	"Nothing . . . shall apply: (a) To the rental of a housing accommodation in a building which contains housing

STATES WHICH EXEMPT OWNER-OCCUPIED DWELLINGS FROM STATE FAIR HOUSING LAWS

(Continued)

State	Exemption for Owner-Occupant	Exemption
		accommodations for not more than two families living independently of each other, if the owner or a member of his family resides in one of the housing accommodations; (b) To the rental of one room or one rooming unit in a housing accommodation by an individual if he or a member of his family resides therein."
LA	Yes	"For purposes of this Section 'housing accommodations' means any real property, or portion thereof, which is used or occupied or is intended, arranged, or designed to be used or occupied, as the home, residence, or sleeping place of one or more human beings, but shall not include any single family residence the occupants of which rent, lease, or furnish for compensation not more than one room therein."
		Also: "Subsection G of this Section [related to the prohibition of discrimination against handicapped persons] shall not apply to the rental of a housing accommodation in a building which contains housing accommodations for two or less units living independently of each other, if the owner resides in one of the housing units, or to the rental of a room or rooms in a single housing dwelling by a per-

STATES WHICH EXEMPT OWNER-OCCUPIED
DWELLINGS FROM STATE FAIR HOUSING LAWS
(Continued)

State	Exemption for Owner-Occupant	Exemption
		son if the lessor or a member of the lessor's immediate family resides therein."
ME	Yes	" 'Housing accommodations' includes any building or structure or portion thereof . . . which is occupied, or is intended to be occupied . . . for residential purposes excepting: A. Two-family dwellings. The rental of a 2-family dwelling, one unit of which is occupied by the owner; B. One-family dwellings. The rental of not more than 4 rooms of a one-family dwelling which is occupied by the owner.
MD	Yes	"With respect to sex discrimination and discrimination on the basis of marital status alone, nothing herein shall be construed to apply to the rental of rooms within any dwelling in which the owner maintains his or her principal residence or to the rental of any apartment in a dwelling containing not more than five units and in which the owner maintains his or her principal residence."
MA	Yes	". . . this subsection shall not apply to the leasing of a single apartment or flat in a two-family dwelling, the other occupancy unit of which is occupied by the owner as his residence."

STATES WHICH EXEMPT OWNER-OCCUPIED DWELLINGS FROM STATE FAIR HOUSING LAWS
(Continued)

State	Exemption for Owner-Occupant	Exemption
MI	Yes	"[This act] . . . shall not apply: (a) to the rental of a housing accommodation in a building which contains housing accommodations for not more than 2 families living independently of each other if the owner or a member of the owner's immediate family resides in one of the housing accommodations, or to the rental of a room or rooms in a single family dwelling by a person if the lessor or a member of the lessor's immediate family resides therein."
MN	Yes	"[The act does not apply to] (b) the rental by an owner or occupier of a one-family accommodation in which he resides of a room or rooms in the accommodation to another person or persons if the discrimination is by sex, marital status, status with regard to public assistance or disability."
MO	Yes	" 'Housing accommodations,' as used in this section [pertaining to equal access to housing accommodations for the blind and visually handicapped] . . . shall not include . . . any single family residence the occupants of which rent, lease, or furnish for compensation not more than one room therein."
MT	Yes	"A private residence designed for single-family occupancy in which sleep-

STATES WHICH EXEMPT OWNER-OCCUPIED
DWELLINGS FROM STATE FAIR HOUSING LAWS
(Continued)

State	Exemption for Owner-Occupant	Exemption
		ing space is rented to guest and in which the landlord resides . . . [is excluded from the act]."
NE	Yes	"Nothing . . . shall prohibit or limit the right of any person or his or her authorized representative to refuse to rent a room or rooms in his or her own home for any reason, or for no reason, or to change tenants in his or her own home as often as desired; *Provided*, that this exception shall not apply to any person who makes available for rental or occupancy more than four sleeping rooms to a person or family within his or her own home."
NH	Yes	"[The act does not apply] (b) To the rental of a housing accommodation in a building which contains housing accommodations for not more than three families living independently of each other, if the owner or members of his family reside in one such housing accommodation; or (c) To the rental of a room or rooms in a housing accommodation if such rental is by the occupant of the housing accommodation and he or members of his family reside in such housing accommodation."
NJ	Yes	". . . the provisions of this act shall not apply to the rental (1) of a single

APPENDIX C

STATES WHICH EXEMPT OWNER-OCCUPIED
DWELLINGS FROM STATE FAIR HOUSING LAWS
(Continued)

State	Exemption for Owner-Occupant	Exemption
		apartment or flat in a 2-family dwelling, the other occupancy unit of which is occupied by the owner as his residence or the household of his family at the time of such rental; or (2) of a room or rooms to another person or persons by the owner or occupant of a one-family dwelling occupied by him as his residence or the household of his family at the time of such rental."
NM	Yes	"Nothing contained in the Human Rights Act shall: (c) apply to rooms or units in dwellings containing living quarters occupied or intended to be occupied by no more than four families living independently of each other, if the owner actually maintains and occupies one of the living quarters as his residence."
NY	Yes	The provisions . . . shall not apply (1) to the rental of a housing accommodation in a building which contains housing accommodations for not more than two families living independently of each other, if the owner or members of his family reside in one of such housing accommodations, (2) to the restriction of the rental of all rooms in a housing accommodation to individuals of the same sex or (3) to the rental of a

117

STATES WHICH EXEMPT OWNER-OCCUPIED
DWELLINGS FROM STATE FAIR HOUSING LAWS
(Continued)

State	Exemption for Owner-Occupant	Exemption
		room or rooms in housing accommodation if such rental is by the occupant of the housing accommodation or by the owner of the housing accommodation and he or members of his family reside in such housing accommodation.
NC	Yes	"The provisions . . . do not apply to . . . (1) The rental of a housing accommodation in a building which contains housing accommodations for not more than four families living independently of each other, if the lessor or a member of his family resides in one of the housing accommodations; (2) The rental of a room or rooms in a house by an individual if he or a member of his family resides therein.
ND	No	None found. State policy against discrimination.
OH	No	None found. Ohio Revised Code Annotated.
OR	No	There is no special exemption for an owner-occupied dwelling. However, the following applies to owners and nonowners alike: "This section [prohibiting discrimination] does not apply with respect to sex distinction, discrimination or restriction if the real property involved is such that the application of this section would

STATES WHICH EXEMPT OWNER-OCCUPIED
DWELLINGS FROM STATE FAIR HOUSING LAWS
(Continued)

State	Exemption for Owner-Occupant	Exemption
		necessarily result in common use of bath or bedroom facilities by unrelated persons of the opposite sex."
PA	Yes	"Nor shall it [the act] apply to the rental of rooms or apartments in a landlord occupied rooming house with a common entrance." And "(K) The term 'personal residence' means a building or structure containing living quarters occupied or intended to be occupied by no more than two individuals, two groups of two families living independently of each other and used by the owner or lessee thereof as a bona fide residence for himself and any members of his family forming his household."
RI	No	None found. Rhode Island Fair Housing Practices Act.
SD	No	None found. State policy against discrimination.
VT	Yes	"This section shall not apply: (1) To the lease of a housing accommodation in a building which contains housing accommodations for not more than two families living independent of each other if the owner or members of his family reside in one of the housing accommodations, or (2) To the rental of not more than four rooms in a housing accommoda-

STATES WHICH EXEMPT OWNER-OCCUPIED
DWELLINGS FROM STATE FAIR HOUSING LAWS
(Continued)

State	Exemption for Owner-Occupant	Exemption
		tion, if the rental is by the occupant of the housing accommodation and he or the members of his family reside therein."
VA	Yes	"Nothing in this act shall apply to . . . rooms or units in dwellings containing living quarters occupied or intended to be occupied by no more than four families living independently of each other, if the owner actually maintains and occupies one of such living quarters as his residence."
WA	No	None found. Law against discrimination.
WV	Yes	"Nothing contained in this definition or this article shall apply to the rental of a room or rooms in a rooming house occupied by the owner as a place of residence and containing no more than four rented rooms, or rooms to be rented."
WI	No	None found. Open housing law.

INDEX

INDEX

Outside entrances, 2
 basement apartments, 12
Owner-occupied houses
 accessory dwelling units in, 2–3
 exempt from state Fair Housing Laws, 13–15, 108–120
Owners; rental forms for, 87–103

Parking for tenant, 2
 complaints about, 3
 off-street, 2
Paying guests, 12
Personal questions, 26–27
Personality or personal property, 67, 82
Plumbing problems, 49
Privacy, 10
 bedrooms and bathrooms, 4–5
Problems, household, 52–53
 boyfriends and/or girlfriends staying over night, 13, 27, 31, 54–55
 energy conservation, 55
 focus on solving, 52, 60
 food supplies, 53–54
 late-paying tenant, 55
 listing household chores, 52–53
 resolving, 60
Property taxes, 66
 deduction allowed, 80
 notices, 62
Public referral services, 19–20
Public transportation services, 4
 bus and/or subway schedules, 9
Purchase contracts, 61

Real estate agents, help in selecting tenant, 20
Receipts, keeping, 63
Record-keeping: advertising expenses, 100
 capital expenditures, 103
 cleaning and maintenance expenses, 100
 documents received at closing, 61–62
 expenses, 99–103
 financial records, 62–63, 81
 Household Information Binder, 61–62, 81–82
 income, 62–65, 94–103
 insurance policies, 62
 IRS requirements, 61–62
 major home improvements, 62
 other expenses, 103
 other income, 98
 receipts, 63
 rental agreements, 61, 92–93, 96
 rents, 96
 repairs, 101
 supplies, 101

Record-keeping (cont.):
 utility expenses, 102
 utility income, 97
 (See also Financial record-keeping)
References, 35–38
 checking with former employer, 37
 checking with former housemates, 37–38
 checking with landlords, 37–38
 referral services, 19–20
 signing rental agreement, 38–39
 Tenant Application Form, 36–37
Referral services, 19–20
 checking out, 20
 fees, 20
 private roommates, 19–20
 public programs, 19–20
 questionnaires, 20
 screening by, 19–20
Rejecting applicant, 32–33
Renovations, 6
Rentability of house, 4–5
 attractiveness, 4–5
 floor plan, 4
 location and, 4
Rental agreements: advance payments, 24, 47–49
 advantages, 41–42
 check for required rent and deposit, 35, 47–49
 checking references, 35–38
 clarity and simplicity in, 41
 clauses, 9, 43–44
 date of tenancy, 46–47
 discussing terms, 22
 fair set of rules, 59
 forms, 44–45, 92–93
 household problems, 52–53
 insurance, 49–51
 late charges, 51, 55
 leases vs., 41–42
 legal obligations, 48
 maintenance and repairs, 49, 100
 month-to-month, 22, 41–42
 open-ended, 41
 owner responsibility, 45
 prohibitions against pets, 51
 record-keeping, 62
 rent increases, 51–52
 restrictions, 4
 rights and responsibilities, 41, 45, 51
 security deposit and first and last month's rent, 35, 38–39, 47–49
 signing, 35, 38–39
 special provisions, 51
 state and local laws, 43, 51
 termination, 42–43, 50–51, 56–59

Index